NIST Special Publication 800-61
Revision 2

Computer Security Incident Handling Guide

Recommendations of the National Institute of Standards and Technology

Paul Cichonski
Computer Security Division
Information Technology Laboratory
National Institute of Standards and Technology
Gaithersburg, MD

Tom Millar
United States Computer Emergency Readiness Team
National Cyber Security Division
Department of Homeland Security

Tim Grance
Computer Security Division
Information Technology Laboratory
National Institute of Standards and Technology
Gaithersburg, MD

Karen Scarfone
Scarfone Cybersecurity

C O M P U T E R   S E C U R I T Y

August 2012

U.S. Department of Commerce

Rebecca Blank, Acting Secretary

National Institute of Standards and Technology

Patrick D. Gallagher,
Under Secretary of Commerce for Standards and Technology
and Director

Reports on Computer Systems Technology

The Information Technology Laboratory (ITL) at the National Institute of Standards and Technology (NIST) promotes the U.S. economy and public welfare by providing technical leadership for the Nation's measurement and standards infrastructure. ITL develops tests, test methods, reference data, proof of concept implementations, and technical analyses to advance the development and productive use of information technology. ITL's responsibilities include the development of management, administrative, technical, and physical standards and guidelines for the cost-effective security and privacy of other than national security-related information in Federal information systems. The Special Publication 800-series reports on ITL's research, guidelines, and outreach efforts in information system security, and its collaborative activities with industry, government, and academic organizations.

Authority

This publication has been developed by NIST to further its statutory responsibilities under the Federal Information Security Management Act (FISMA), Public Law (P.L.) 107-347. NIST is responsible for developing information security standards and guidelines, including minimum requirements for Federal information systems, but such standards and guidelines shall not apply to national security systems without the express approval of appropriate Federal officials exercising policy authority over such systems. This guideline is consistent with the requirements of the Office of Management and Budget (OMB) Circular A-130, Section 8b(3), *Securing Agency Information Systems*, as analyzed in Circular A-130, Appendix IV: *Analysis of Key Sections*. Supplemental information is provided in Circular A-130, Appendix III, *Security of Federal Automated Information Resources*.

Nothing in this publication should be taken to contradict the standards and guidelines made mandatory and binding on Federal agencies by the Secretary of Commerce under statutory authority. Nor should these guidelines be interpreted as altering or superseding the existing authorities of the Secretary of Commerce, Director of the OMB, or any other Federal official. This publication may be used by nongovernmental organizations on a voluntary basis and is not subject to copyright in the United States. Attribution would, however, be appreciated by NIST.

Comments on this publication may be submitted to:

National Institute of Standards and Technology
Attn: Computer Security Division, Information Technology Laboratory
100 Bureau Drive (Mail Stop 8930), Gaithersburg, MD 20899-8930

Abstract

Computer security incident response has become an important component of information technology (IT) programs. Because performing incident response effectively is a complex undertaking, establishing a successful incident response capability requires substantial planning and resources. This publication assists organizations in establishing computer security incident response capabilities and handling incidents efficiently and effectively. This publication provides guidelines for incident handling, particularly for analyzing incident-related data and determining the appropriate response to each incident. The guidelines can be followed independently of particular hardware platforms, operating systems, protocols, or applications.

Keywords

computer security incident; incident handling; incident response; information security

Acknowledgments

The authors, Paul Cichonski of the National Institute of Standards and Technology (NIST), Tom Millar of the United States Computer Emergency Readiness Team (US-CERT), Tim Grance of NIST, and Karen Scarfone of Scarfone Cybersecurity wish to thank their colleagues who reviewed drafts of this document and contributed to its technical content, including John Banghart of NIST; Brian Allen, Mark Austin, Brian DeWyngaert, Andrew Fuller, Chris Hallenbeck, Sharon Kim, Mischel Kwon, Lee Rock, Richard Struse, and Randy Vickers of US-CERT; and Marcos Osorno of the Johns Hopkins University Applied Physics Laboratory. A special acknowledgment goes to Brent Logan of US-CERT for his graphics assistance. The authors would also like to thank security experts Simon Burson, Anton Chuvakin (Gartner), Fred Cohen (Fred Cohen & Associates), Mariano M. del Rio (SIClabs), Jake Evans (Tripwire), Walter Houser (SRA), Panos Kampanakis (Cisco), Kathleen Moriarty (EMC), David Schwalenberg (National Security Agency), and Wes Young (Research and Education Networking Information Sharing and Analysis Center [REN-ISAC]), as well as representatives of the Blue Glacier Management Group, the Centers for Disease Control and Prevention, the Department of Energy, the Department of State, and the Federal Aviation Administration for their particularly valuable comments and suggestions.

The authors would also like to acknowledge the individuals that contributed to the previous versions of the publication. A special thanks goes to Brian Kim of Booz Allen Hamilton, who co-authored the original version; to Kelly Masone of Blue Glacier Management Group, who co-authored the first revision; and also to Rick Ayers, Chad Bloomquist, Vincent Hu, Peter Mell, Scott Rose, Murugiah Souppaya, Gary Stoneburner, and John Wack of NIST; Don Benack and Mike Witt of US-CERT; and Debra Banning, Pete Coleman, Alexis Feringa, Tracee Glass, Kevin Kuhlkin, Bryan Laird, Chris Manteuffel, Ron Ritchey, and Marc Stevens of Booz Allen Hamilton for their keen and insightful assistance throughout the development of the document, as well as Ron Banerjee and Gene Schultz for their work on a preliminary draft of the document. The authors would also like to express their thanks to security experts Tom Baxter (NASA), Mark Bruhn (Indiana University), Brian Carrier (CERIAS, Purdue University), Eoghan Casey, Johnny Davis, Jr. (Department of Veterans Affairs), Jim Duncan (BB&T), Dean Farrington (Wells Fargo Bank), John Hale (University of Tulsa), Georgia Killcrece (CERT®/CC), Barbara Laswell (CERT®/CC), Pascal Meunier (CERIAS, Purdue University), Jeff Murphy (University of Buffalo), Todd O'Boyle (MITRE), Marc Rogers (CERIAS, Purdue University), Steve Romig (Ohio State University), Robin Ruefle (CERT®/CC), Gene Schultz (Lawrence Berkeley National Laboratory), Michael Smith (US-CERT), Holt Sorenson, Eugene Spafford (CERIAS, Purdue University), Ken van Wyk, and Mark Zajicek (CERT®/CC), as well as representatives of the Department of the Treasury, for their particularly valuable comments and suggestions.

Table of Contents

List of Appendices

List of Figures

List of Tables

Executive Summary

Computer security incident response has become an important component of information technology (IT) programs. Cybersecurity-related attacks have become not only more numerous and diverse but also more damaging and disruptive. New types of security-related incidents emerge frequently. Preventive activities based on the results of risk assessments can lower the number of incidents, but not all incidents can be prevented. An incident response capability is therefore necessary for rapidly detecting incidents, minimizing loss and destruction, mitigating the weaknesses that were exploited, and restoring IT services. To that end, this publication provides guidelines for incident handling, particularly for analyzing incident-related data and determining the appropriate response to each incident. The guidelines can be followed independently of particular hardware platforms, operating systems, protocols, or applications.

Because performing incident response effectively is a complex undertaking, establishing a successful incident response capability requires substantial planning and resources. Continually monitoring for attacks is essential. Establishing clear procedures for prioritizing the handling of incidents is critical, as is implementing effective methods of collecting, analyzing, and reporting data. It is also vital to build relationships and establish suitable means of communication with other internal groups (e.g., human resources, legal) and with external groups (e.g., other incident response teams, law enforcement).

This publication assists organizations in establishing computer security incident response capabilities and handling incidents efficiently and effectively. This revision of the publication, Revision 2, updates material throughout the publication to reflect the changes in attacks and incidents. Understanding threats and identifying modern attacks in their early stages is key to preventing subsequent compromises, and proactively sharing information among organizations regarding the signs of these attacks is an increasingly effective way to identify them.

Implementing the following requirements and recommendations should facilitate efficient and effective incident response for Federal departments and agencies.

Organizations must create, provision, and operate a formal incident response capability. Federal law requires Federal agencies to report incidents to the United States Computer Emergency Readiness Team (US-CERT) office within the Department of Homeland Security (DHS).

The Federal Information Security Management Act (FISMA) requires Federal agencies to establish incident response capabilities. Each Federal civilian agency must designate a primary and secondary point of contact (POC) with US-CERT and report all incidents consistent with the agency's incident response policy. Each agency is responsible for determining how to fulfill these requirements.

Establishing an incident response capability should include the following actions:

- Creating an incident response policy and plan
- Developing procedures for performing incident handling and reporting
- Setting guidelines for communicating with outside parties regarding incidents
- Selecting a team structure and staffing model
- Establishing relationships and lines of communication between the incident response team and other groups, both internal (e.g., legal department) and external (e.g., law enforcement agencies)
- Determining what services the incident response team should provide

- Staffing and training the incident response team.

Organizations should reduce the frequency of incidents by effectively securing networks, systems, and applications.

Preventing problems is often less costly and more effective than reacting to them after they occur. Thus, incident prevention is an important complement to an incident response capability. If security controls are insufficient, high volumes of incidents may occur. This could overwhelm the resources and capacity for response, which would result in delayed or incomplete recovery and possibly more extensive damage and longer periods of service and data unavailability. Incident handling can be performed more effectively if organizations complement their incident response capability with adequate resources to actively maintain the security of networks, systems, and applications. This includes training IT staff on complying with the organization's security standards and making users aware of policies and procedures regarding appropriate use of networks, systems, and applications.

Organizations should document their guidelines for interactions with other organizations regarding incidents.

During incident handling, the organization will need to communicate with outside parties, such as other incident response teams, law enforcement, the media, vendors, and victim organizations. Because these communications often need to occur quickly, organizations should predetermine communication guidelines so that only the appropriate information is shared with the right parties.

Organizations should be generally prepared to handle any incident but should focus on being prepared to handle incidents that use common attack vectors.

Incidents can occur in countless ways, so it is infeasible to develop step-by-step instructions for handling every incident. This publication defines several types of incidents, based on common attack vectors; these categories are not intended to provide definitive classification for incidents, but rather to be used as a basis for defining more specific handling procedures. Different types of incidents merit different response strategies. The attack vectors are:

- **External/Removable Media:** An attack executed from removable media (e.g., flash drive, CD) or a peripheral device.
- **Attrition:** An attack that employs brute force methods to compromise, degrade, or destroy systems, networks, or services.
- **Web:** An attack executed from a website or web-based application.
- **Email:** An attack executed via an email message or attachment.
- **Improper Usage:** Any incident resulting from violation of an organization's acceptable usage policies by an authorized user, excluding the above categories.
- **Loss or Theft of Equipment:** The loss or theft of a computing device or media used by the organization, such as a laptop or smartphone.
- **Other:** An attack that does not fit into any of the other categories.

Organizations should emphasize the importance of incident detection and analysis throughout the organization.

In an organization, millions of possible signs of incidents may occur each day, recorded mainly by logging and computer security software. Automation is needed to perform an initial analysis of the data and select events of interest for human review. Event correlation software can be of great value in automating the analysis process. However, the effectiveness of the process depends on the quality of the data that goes into it. Organizations should establish logging standards and procedures to ensure that adequate information is collected by logs and security software and that the data is reviewed regularly.

Organizations should create written guidelines for prioritizing incidents.

Prioritizing the handling of individual incidents is a critical decision point in the incident response process. Effective information sharing can help an organization identify situations that are of greater severity and demand immediate attention. Incidents should be prioritized based on the relevant factors, such as the functional impact of the incident (e.g., current and likely future negative impact to business functions), the information impact of the incident (e.g., effect on the confidentiality, integrity, and availability of the organization's information), and the recoverability from the incident (e.g., the time and types of resources that must be spent on recovering from the incident).

Organizations should use the lessons learned process to gain value from incidents.

After a major incident has been handled, the organization should hold a lessons learned meeting to review the effectiveness of the incident handling process and identify necessary improvements to existing security controls and practices. Lessons learned meetings can also be held periodically for lesser incidents as time and resources permit. The information accumulated from all lessons learned meetings should be used to identify and correct systemic weaknesses and deficiencies in policies and procedures. Follow-up reports generated for each resolved incident can be important not only for evidentiary purposes but also for reference in handling future incidents and in training new team members.

1. Introduction

1.1 Authority

The National Institute of Standards and Technology (NIST) developed this document in furtherance of its statutory responsibilities under the Federal Information Security Management Act (FISMA) of 2002, Public Law 107-347.

NIST is responsible for developing standards and guidelines, including minimum requirements, for providing adequate information security for all agency operations and assets, but such standards and guidelines shall not apply to national security systems. This guideline is consistent with the requirements of the Office of Management and Budget (OMB) Circular A-130, Section 8b(3), "Securing Agency Information Systems," as analyzed in A-130, Appendix IV: Analysis of Key Sections. Supplemental information is provided in A-130, Appendix III.

This guideline has been prepared for use by Federal agencies. It may be used by nongovernmental organizations on a voluntary basis and is not subject to copyright, though attribution is desired.

Nothing in this document should be taken to contradict standards and guidelines made mandatory and binding on Federal agencies by the Secretary of Commerce under statutory authority, nor should these guidelines be interpreted as altering or superseding the existing authorities of the Secretary of Commerce, Director of the OMB, or any other Federal official.

1.2 Purpose and Scope

This publication seeks to assist organizations in mitigating the risks from computer security incidents by providing practical guidelines on responding to incidents effectively and efficiently. It includes guidelines on establishing an effective incident response program, but the primary focus of the document is detecting, analyzing, prioritizing, and handling incidents. Organizations are encouraged to tailor the recommended guidelines and solutions to meet their specific security and mission requirements.

1.3 Audience

This document has been created for computer security incident response teams (CSIRTs), system and network administrators, security staff, technical support staff, chief information security officers (CISOs), chief information officers (CIOs), computer security program managers, and others who are responsible for preparing for, or responding to, security incidents.

1.4 Document Structure

The remainder of this document is organized into the following sections and appendices:

- Section 2 discusses the need for incident response, outlines possible incident response team structures, and highlights other groups within an organization that may participate in incident handling.
- Section 3 reviews the basic incident handling steps and provides advice for performing incident handling more effectively, particularly incident detection and analysis.
- Section 4 examines the need for incident response coordination and information sharing.

- Appendix A contains incident response scenarios and questions for use in incident response tabletop discussions.
- Appendix B provides lists of suggested data fields to collect for each incident.
- Appendices C and D contain a glossary and acronym list, respectively.
- Appendix E identifies resources that may be useful in planning and performing incident response.
- Appendix F covers frequently asked questions about incident response.
- Appendix G lists the major steps to follow when handling a computer security incident-related crisis.
- Appendix H contains a change log listing significant changes since the previous revision.

2. Organizing a Computer Security Incident Response Capability

Organizing an effective computer security incident response capability (CSIRC) involves several major decisions and actions. One of the first considerations should be to create an organization-specific definition of the term "incident" so that the scope of the term is clear. The organization should decide what services the incident response team should provide, consider which team structures and models can provide those services, and select and implement one or more incident response teams. Incident response plan, policy, and procedure creation is an important part of establishing a team, so that incident response is performed effectively, efficiently, and consistently, and so that the team is empowered to do what needs to be done. The plan, policies, and procedures should reflect the team's interactions with other teams within the organization as well as with outside parties, such as law enforcement, the media, and other incident response organizations. This section provides not only guidelines that should be helpful to organizations that are establishing incident response capabilities, but also advice on maintaining and enhancing existing capabilities.

2.1 Events and Incidents

An *event* is any observable occurrence in a system or network. Events include a user connecting to a file share, a server receiving a request for a web page, a user sending email, and a firewall blocking a connection attempt. *Adverse events* are events with a negative consequence, such as system crashes, packet floods, unauthorized use of system privileges, unauthorized access to sensitive data, and execution of malware that destroys data. This guide addresses only adverse events that are computer security-related, not those caused by natural disasters, power failures, etc.

A *computer security incident* is a violation or imminent threat of violation[1] of computer security policies, acceptable use policies, or standard security practices. Examples of incidents[2] are:

- An attacker commands a botnet to send high volumes of connection requests to a web server, causing it to crash.
- Users are tricked into opening a "quarterly report" sent via email that is actually malware; running the tool has infected their computers and established connections with an external host.
- An attacker obtains sensitive data and threatens that the details will be released publicly if the organization does not pay a designated sum of money.
- A user provides or exposes sensitive information to others through peer-to-peer file sharing services.

2.2 Need for Incident Response

Attacks frequently compromise personal and business data, and it is critical to respond quickly and effectively when security breaches occur. The concept of computer security incident response has become widely accepted and implemented. One of the benefits of having an incident response capability is that it supports responding to incidents systematically (i.e., following a consistent incident handling methodology) so that the appropriate actions are taken. Incident response helps personnel to minimize loss or theft of information and disruption of services caused by incidents. Another benefit of incident response is the ability to use information gained during incident handling to better prepare for handling

---

1 An "imminent threat of violation" refers to a situation in which the organization has a factual basis for believing that a specific incident is about to occur. For example, the antivirus software maintainers may receive a bulletin from the software vendor, warning them of new malware that is rapidly spreading across the Internet.

2 For the remainder of this document, the terms "incident" and "computer security incident" are interchangeable.

future incidents and to provide stronger protection for systems and data. An incident response capability also helps with dealing properly with legal issues that may arise during incidents.

Besides the business reasons to establish an incident response capability, Federal departments and agencies must comply with law, regulations, and policy directing a coordinated, effective defense against information security threats. Chief among these are the following:

- OMB's Circular No. A-130, Appendix III,[3] released in 2000, which directs Federal agencies to "ensure that there is a capability to provide help to users when a security incident occurs in the system and to share information concerning common vulnerabilities and threats. This capability shall share information with other organizations … and should assist the agency in pursuing appropriate legal action, consistent with Department of Justice guidance."
- FISMA (from 2002),[4] which requires agencies to have "procedures for detecting, reporting, and responding to security incidents" and establishes a centralized Federal information security incident center, in part to:
  - "Provide timely technical assistance to operators of agency information systems … including guidance on detecting and handling information security incidents …
  - Compile and analyze information about incidents that threaten information security …
  - Inform operators of agency information systems about current and potential information security threats, and vulnerabilities … ."
- Federal Information Processing Standards (FIPS) 200, *Minimum Security Requirements for Federal Information and Information Systems*[5], March 2006, which specifies minimum security requirements for Federal information and information systems, including incident response. The specific requirements are defined in NIST Special Publication (SP) 800-53, *Recommended Security Controls for Federal Information Systems and Organizations*.
- OMB Memorandum M-07-16, *Safeguarding Against and Responding to the Breach of Personally Identifiable Information*[6], May 2007, which provides guidance on reporting security incidents that involve PII.

2.3 Incident Response Policy, Plan, and Procedure Creation

This section discusses policies, plans, and procedures related to incident response, with an emphasis on interactions with outside parties.

2.3.1 Policy Elements

Policy governing incident response is highly individualized to the organization. However, most policies include the same key elements:

- Statement of management commitment
- Purpose and objectives of the policy

---

3 http://www.whitehouse.gov/omb/circulars/a130/a130trans4 html
4 http://csrc nist.gov/drivers/documents/FISMA-final.pdf
5 http://csrc nist.gov/publications/PubsFIPS html
6 http://www.whitehouse.gov/omb/memoranda/fy2007/m07-16.pdf

- Scope of the policy (to whom and what it applies and under what circumstances)
- Definition of computer security incidents and related terms
- Organizational structure and definition of roles, responsibilities, and levels of authority; should include the authority of the incident response team to confiscate or disconnect equipment and to monitor suspicious activity, the requirements for reporting certain types of incidents, the requirements and guidelines for external communications and information sharing (e.g., what can be shared with whom, when, and over what channels), and the handoff and escalation points in the incident management process
- Prioritization or severity ratings of incidents
- Performance measures (as discussed in Section 3.4.2)
- Reporting and contact forms.

2.3.2 Plan Elements

Organizations should have a formal, focused, and coordinated approach to responding to incidents, including an incident response plan that provides the roadmap for implementing the incident response capability. Each organization needs a plan that meets its unique requirements, which relates to the organization's mission, size, structure, and functions. The plan should lay out the necessary resources and management support. The incident response plan should include the following elements:

- Mission
- Strategies and goals
- Senior management approval
- Organizational approach to incident response
- How the incident response team will communicate with the rest of the organization and with other organizations
- Metrics for measuring the incident response capability and its effectiveness
- Roadmap for maturing the incident response capability
- How the program fits into the overall organization.

The organization's mission, strategies, and goals for incident response should help in determining the structure of its incident response capability. The incident response program structure should also be discussed within the plan. Section 2.4.1 discusses the types of structures.

Once an organization develops a plan and gains management approval, the organization should implement the plan and review it at least annually to ensure the organization is following the roadmap for maturing the capability and fulfilling their goals for incident response.

2.3.3 Procedure Elements

Procedures should be based on the incident response policy and plan. Standard operating procedures (SOPs) are a delineation of the specific technical processes, techniques, checklists, and forms used by the incident response team. SOPs should be reasonably comprehensive and detailed to ensure that the priorities of the organization are reflected in response operations. In addition, following standardized responses should minimize errors, particularly those that might be caused by stressful incident handling situations. SOPs should be tested to validate their accuracy and usefulness, then distributed to all team members. Training should be provided for SOP users; the SOP documents can be used as an instructional tool. Suggested SOP elements are presented throughout Section 3.

2.3.4 Sharing Information With Outside Parties

Organizations often need to communicate with outside parties regarding an incident, and they should do so whenever appropriate, such as contacting law enforcement, fielding media inquiries, and seeking external expertise. Another example is discussing incidents with other involved parties, such as Internet service providers (ISPs), the vendor of vulnerable software, or other incident response teams. Organizations may also proactively share relevant incident indicator information with peers to improve detection and analysis of incidents. The incident response team should discuss information sharing with the organization's public affairs office, legal department, and management before an incident occurs to establish policies and procedures regarding information sharing. Otherwise, sensitive information regarding incidents may be provided to unauthorized parties, potentially leading to additional disruption and financial loss. The team should document all contacts and communications with outside parties for liability and evidentiary purposes.

The following sections provide guidelines on communicating with several types of outside parties, as depicted in Figure 2-1. The double-headed arrows indicate that either party may initiate communications. See Section 4 for additional information on communicating with outside parties, and see Section 2.4 for a discussion of communications involving incident response outsourcers.

Figure 2-1. Communications with Outside Parties

2.3.4.1 The Media

The incident handling team should establish media communications procedures that comply with the organization's policies on media interaction and information disclosure.[7] For discussing incidents with the media, organizations often find it beneficial to designate a single point of contact (POC) and at least one backup contact. The following actions are recommended for preparing these designated contacts and should also be considered for preparing others who may be communicating with the media:

- Conduct training sessions on interacting with the media regarding incidents, which should include the importance of not revealing sensitive information, such as technical details of countermeasures that could assist other attackers, and the positive aspects of communicating important information to the public fully and effectively.
- Establish procedures to brief media contacts on the issues and sensitivities regarding a particular incident before discussing it with the media.

[7] For example, an organization may want members of its public affairs office and legal department to participate in all incident discussions with the media.

- Maintain a statement of the current status of the incident so that communications with the media are consistent and up-to-date.
- Remind all staff of the general procedures for handling media inquiries.
- Hold mock interviews and press conferences during incident handling exercises. The following are examples of questions to ask the media contact:
  - Who attacked you? Why?
  - When did it happen? How did it happen? Did this happen because you have poor security practices?
  - How widespread is this incident? What steps are you taking to determine what happened and to prevent future occurrences?
  - What is the impact of this incident? Was any personally identifiable information (PII) exposed? What is the estimated cost of this incident?

2.3.4.2 Law Enforcement

One reason that many security-related incidents do not result in convictions is that some organizations do not properly contact law enforcement. Several levels of law enforcement are available to investigate incidents: for example, within the United States, Federal investigatory agencies (e.g., the Federal Bureau of Investigation [FBI] and the U.S. Secret Service), district attorney offices, state law enforcement, and local (e.g., county) law enforcement. Law enforcement agencies in other countries may also be involved, such as for attacks launched from or directed at locations outside the US. In addition, agencies have an Office of Inspector General (OIG) for investigation of violation of the law within each agency. The incident response team should become acquainted with its various law enforcement representatives before an incident occurs to discuss conditions under which incidents should be reported to them, how the reporting should be performed, what evidence should be collected, and how it should be collected.

Law enforcement should be contacted through designated individuals in a manner consistent with the requirements of the law and the organization's procedures. Many organizations prefer to appoint one incident response team member as the primary POC with law enforcement. This person should be familiar with the reporting procedures for all relevant law enforcement agencies and well prepared to recommend which agency, if any, should be contacted. Note that the organization typically should not contact multiple agencies because doing so might result in jurisdictional conflicts. The incident response team should understand what the potential jurisdictional issues are (e.g., physical location—an organization based in one state has a server located in a second state attacked from a system in a third state, being used remotely by an attacker in a fourth state).

2.3.4.3 Incident Reporting Organizations

FISMA requires Federal agencies to report incidents to the United States Computer Emergency Readiness Team (US-CERT),[8] which is a governmentwide incident response organization that assists Federal civilian agencies in their incident handling efforts. US-CERT does not replace existing agency response teams; rather, it augments the efforts of Federal civilian agencies by serving as a focal point for dealing with incidents. US-CERT analyzes the agency-provided information to identify trends and indicators of attacks; these are easier to discern when reviewing data from many organizations than when reviewing the data of a single organization.

---

8 http://www.us-cert.gov/

Each agency must designate a primary and secondary POC with US-CERT and report all incidents consistent with the agency's incident response policy. Organizations should create a policy that states who is designated to report incidents and how the incidents should be reported. Requirements, categories, and timeframes for reporting incidents to US-CERT are on the US-CERT website.[9] All Federal agencies must ensure that their incident response procedures adhere to US-CERT's reporting requirements and that the procedures are followed properly.

All organizations are encouraged to report incidents to their appropriate CSIRTs. If an organization does not have its own CSIRT to contact, it can report incidents to other organizations, including Information Sharing and Analysis Centers (ISACs). One of the functions of these industry-specific private sector groups is to share important computer security-related information among their members. Several ISACs have been formed for industry sectors such as Communications, Electric Sector, Financial Services, Information Technology, and Research and Education.[10]

2.3.4.4 Other Outside Parties

An organization may want to discuss incidents with other groups, including those listed below. When reaching out to these external parties, an organization may want to work through US-CERT or its ISAC, as a "trusted introducer" to broker the relationship. It is likely that others are experiencing similar issues, and the trusted introducer can ensure that any such patterns are identified and taken into consideration.

- **Organization's ISP.** An organization may need assistance from its ISP in blocking a major network-based attack or tracing its origin.
- **Owners of Attacking Addresses.** If attacks are originating from an external organization's IP address space, incident handlers may want to talk to the designated security contacts for the organization to alert them to the activity or to ask them to collect evidence. It is highly recommended to coordinate such communications with US-CERT or an ISAC.
- **Software Vendors.** Incident handlers may want to speak to a software vendor about suspicious activity. This contact could include questions regarding the significance of certain log entries or known false positives for certain intrusion detection signatures, where minimal information regarding the incident may need to be revealed. More information may need to be provided in some cases—for example, if a server appears to have been compromised through an unknown software vulnerability. Software vendors may also provide information on known threats (e.g., new attacks) to help organizations understand the current threat environment.
- **Other Incident Response Teams.** An organization may experience an incident that is similar to ones handled by other teams; proactively sharing information can facilitate more effective and efficient incident handling (e.g., providing advance warning, increasing preparedness, developing situational awareness). Groups such as the Forum of Incident Response and Security Teams (FIRST)[11], the Government Forum of Incident Response and Security Teams (GFIRST)[12], and the Anti-Phishing Working Group (APWG)[13] are not incident response teams, but they promote information sharing among incident response teams.
- **Affected External Parties.** An incident may affect external parties directly—for example, an outside organization may contact the organization and claim that one of the organization's users is attacking

9 http://www.us-cert.gov/federal/reportingRequirements.html
10 See the National Council of ISACs website at http://www.isaccouncil.org/ for a list of ISACs.
11 http://www.first.org/
12 GFIRST is specifically for Federal departments and agencies. (http://www.us-cert.gov/federal/gfirst.html)
13 http://www.antiphishing.org/

it. Another way in which external parties may be affected is if an attacker gains access to sensitive information regarding them, such as credit card information. In some jurisdictions, organizations are required to notify all parties that are affected by such an incident. Regardless of the circumstances, it is preferable for the organization to notify affected external parties of an incident before the media or other external organizations do so. Handlers should be careful to give out only appropriate information—the affected parties may request details about internal investigations that should not be revealed publicly.

OMB Memorandum M-07-16, *Safeguarding Against and Responding to the Breach of Personally Identifiable Information*, requires Federal agencies to develop and implement a breach notification policy for personally identifiable information (PII).[14] Incident handlers should understand how their incident handling actions should differ when a PII breach is suspected to have occurred, such as notifying additional parties or notifying parties within a shorter timeframe. Specific recommendations for PII breach notification policies are presented in OMB Memorandum M-07-16. Also, the National Conference of State Legislatures has a list of state security breach notification laws.[15]

2.4 Incident Response Team Structure

An incident response team should be available for anyone who discovers or suspects that an incident involving the organization has occurred. One or more team members, depending on the magnitude of the incident and availability of personnel, will then handle the incident. The incident handlers analyze the incident data, determine the impact of the incident, and act appropriately to limit the damage and restore normal services. The incident response team's success depends on the participation and cooperation of individuals throughout the organization. This section identifies such individuals, discusses incident response team models, and provides advice on selecting an appropriate model.

2.4.1 Team Models

Possible structures for an incident response team include the following:

- **Central Incident Response Team.** A single incident response team handles incidents throughout the organization. This model is effective for small organizations and for organizations with minimal geographic diversity in terms of computing resources.
- **Distributed Incident Response Teams.** The organization has multiple incident response teams, each responsible for a particular logical or physical segment of the organization. This model is effective for large organizations (e.g., one team per division) and for organizations with major computing resources at distant locations (e.g., one team per geographic region, one team per major facility). However, the teams should be part of a single coordinated entity so that the incident response process is consistent across the organization and information is shared among teams. This is particularly important because multiple teams may see components of the same incident or may handle similar incidents.
- **Coordinating Team.** An incident response team provides advice to other teams without having authority over those teams—for example, a departmentwide team may assist individual agencies' teams. This model can be thought of as a CSIRT for CSIRTs. Because the focus of this document is

[14] http://www.whitehouse.gov/omb/memoranda/fy2007/m07-16.pdf
[15] http://www.ncsl.org/default.aspx?tabid=13489

central and distributed CSIRTs, the coordinating team model is not addressed in detail in this document.[16]

Incident response teams can also use any of three staffing models:

- **Employees.** The organization performs all of its incident response work, with limited technical and administrative support from contractors.
- **Partially Outsourced.** The organization outsources portions of its incident response work. Section 2.4.2 discusses the major factors that should be considered with outsourcing. Although incident response duties can be divided among the organization and one or more outsourcers in many ways, a few arrangements have become commonplace:
  - The most prevalent arrangement is for the organization to outsource 24-hours-a-day, 7-days-a-week (24/7) monitoring of intrusion detection sensors, firewalls, and other security devices to an offsite managed security services provider (MSSP). The MSSP identifies and analyzes suspicious activity and reports each detected incident to the organization's incident response team.
  - Some organizations perform basic incident response work in-house and call on contractors to assist with handling incidents, particularly those that are more serious or widespread.
- **Fully Outsourced.** The organization completely outsources its incident response work, typically to an onsite contractor. This model is most likely to be used when the organization needs a full-time, onsite incident response team but does not have enough available, qualified employees. It is assumed that the organization will have employees supervising and overseeing the outsourcer's work.

2.4.2 Team Model Selection

When selecting appropriate structure and staffing models for an incident response team, organizations should consider the following factors:

- **The Need for 24/7 Availability.** Most organizations need incident response staff to be available 24/7. This typically means that incident handlers can be contacted by phone, but it can also mean that an onsite presence is required. Real-time availability is the best for incident response because the longer an incident lasts, the more potential there is for damage and loss. Real-time contact is often needed when working with other organizations—for example, tracing an attack back to its source.
- **Full-Time Versus Part-Time Team Members.** Organizations with limited funding, staffing, or incident response needs may have only part-time incident response team members, serving as more of a virtual incident response team. In this case, the incident response team can be thought of as a volunteer fire department. When an emergency occurs, the team members are contacted rapidly, and those who can assist do so. An existing group such as the IT help desk can act as a first POC for incident reporting. The help desk members can be trained to perform the initial investigation and data gathering and then alert the incident response team if it appears that a serious incident has occurred.
- **Employee Morale.** Incident response work is very stressful, as are the on-call responsibilities of most team members. This combination makes it easy for incident response team members to become overly stressed. Many organizations will also struggle to find willing, available, experienced, and properly skilled people to participate, particularly in 24-hour support. Segregating roles, particularly

[16] Information about the Coordinating team model, as well as extensive information on other team models, is available in a CERT®/CC document titled *Organizational Models for Computer Security Incident Response Teams (CSIRTs)* (http://www.cert.org/archive/pdf/03hb001.pdf).

reducing the amount of administrative work that team members are responsible for performing, can be a significant boost to morale.

- **Cost.** Cost is a major factor, especially if employees are required to be onsite 24/7. Organizations may fail to include incident response-specific costs in budgets, such as sufficient funding for training and maintaining skills. Because the incident response team works with so many facets of IT, its members need much broader knowledge than most IT staff members. They must also understand how to use the tools of incident response, such as digital forensics software. Other costs that may be overlooked are physical security for the team's work areas and communications mechanisms.
- **Staff Expertise.** Incident handling requires specialized knowledge and experience in several technical areas; the breadth and depth of knowledge required varies based on the severity of the organization's risks. Outsourcers may possess deeper knowledge of intrusion detection, forensics, vulnerabilities, exploits, and other aspects of security than employees of the organization. Also, MSSPs may be able to correlate events among customers so that they can identify new threats more quickly than any individual customer could. However, technical staff members within the organization usually have much better knowledge of the organization's environment than an outsourcer would, which can be beneficial in identifying false positives associated with organization-specific behavior and the criticality of targets. Section 2.4.3 contains additional information on recommended team member skills.

When considering outsourcing, organizations should keep these issues in mind:

- **Current and Future Quality of Work.** Organizations should consider not only the current quality (breadth and depth) of the outsourcer's work, but also efforts to ensure the quality of future work—for example, minimizing turnover and burnout and providing a solid training program for new employees. Organizations should think about how they could objectively assess the quality of the outsourcer's work.
- **Division of Responsibilities.** Organizations are often unwilling to give an outsourcer authority to make operational decisions for the environment (e.g., disconnecting a web server). It is important to document the appropriate actions for these decision points. For example, one partially outsourced model addresses this issue by having the outsourcer provide incident data to the organization's internal team, along with recommendations for further handling the incident. The internal team ultimately makes the operational decisions, with the outsourcer continuing to provide support as needed.
- **Sensitive Information Revealed to the Contractor.** Dividing incident response responsibilities and restricting access to sensitive information can limit this. For example, a contractor may determine what user ID was used in an incident (e.g., ID 123456) but not know what person is associated with the user ID. Employees can then take over the investigation. Non-disclosure agreements (NDAs) are one possible option for protecting the disclosure of sensitive information.
- **Lack of Organization-Specific Knowledge.** Accurate analysis and prioritization of incidents are dependent on specific knowledge of the organization's environment. The organization should provide the outsourcer regularly updated documents that define what incidents it is concerned about, which resources are critical, and what the level of response should be under various sets of circumstances. The organization should also report all changes and updates made to its IT infrastructure, network configuration, and systems. Otherwise, the contractor has to make a best guess as to how each incident should be handled, inevitably leading to mishandled incidents and frustration on both sides. Lack of organization-specific knowledge can also be a problem when incident response is not outsourced if communications are weak among teams or if the organization simply does not collect the necessary information.

- **Lack of Correlation.** Correlation among multiple data sources is very important. If the intrusion detection system records an attempted attack against a web server, but the outsourcer has no access to the server's logs, it may be unable to determine whether the attack was successful. To be efficient, the outsourcer will require administrative privileges to critical systems and security device logs remotely over a secure channel. This will increase administration costs, introduce additional access entry points, and increase the risk of unauthorized disclosure of sensitive information.
- **Handling Incidents at Multiple Locations.** Effective incident response work often requires a physical presence at the organization's facilities. If the outsourcer is offsite, consider where the outsourcer is located, how quickly it can have an incident response team at any facility, and how much this will cost. Consider onsite visits; perhaps there are certain facilities or areas where the outsourcer should not be permitted to work.
- **Maintaining Incident Response Skills In-House.** Organizations that completely outsource incident response should strive to maintain basic incident response skills in-house. Situations may arise in which the outsourcer is unavailable, so the organization should be prepared to perform its own incident handling. The organization's technical staff must also be able to understand the significance, technical implications, and impact of the outsourcer's recommendations.

2.4.3 Incident Response Personnel

A single employee, with one or more designated alternates, should be in charge of incident response. In a fully outsourced model, this person oversees and evaluates the outsourcer's work. All other models generally have a team manager and one or more deputies who assumes authority in the absence of the team manager. The managers typically perform a variety of tasks, including acting as a liaison with upper management and other teams and organizations, defusing crisis situations, and ensuring that the team has the necessary personnel, resources, and skills. Managers should be technically adept and have excellent communication skills, particularly an ability to communicate to a range of audiences. Managers are ultimately responsible for ensuring that incident response activities are performed properly.

In addition to the team manager and deputy, some teams also have a technical lead—a person with strong technical skills and incident response experience who assumes oversight of and final responsibility for the quality of the team's technical work. The position of technical lead should not be confused with the position of incident lead. Larger teams often assign an incident lead as the primary POC for handling a specific incident; the incident lead is held accountable for the incident's handling. Depending on the size of the incident response team and the magnitude of the incident, the incident lead may not actually perform any actual incident handling, but rather coordinate the handlers' activities, gather information from the handlers, provide incident updates to other groups, and ensure that the team's needs are met.

Members of the incident response team should have excellent technical skills, such as system administration, network administration, programming, technical support, or intrusion detection. Every team member should have good problem solving skills and critical thinking abilities. It is not necessary for every team member to be a technical expert—to a large degree, practical and funding considerations will dictate this—but having at least one highly proficient person in each major area of technology (e.g., commonly attacked operating systems and applications) is a necessity. It may also be helpful to have some team members specialize in particular technical areas, such as network intrusion detection, malware analysis, or forensics. It is also often helpful to temporarily bring in technical specialists that aren't normally part of the team.

It is important to counteract staff burnout by providing opportunities for learning and growth. Suggestions for building and maintaining skills are as follows:

- Budget enough funding to maintain, enhance, and expand proficiency in technical areas and security disciplines, as well as less technical topics such as the legal aspects of incident response. This should include sending staff to conferences and encouraging or otherwise incentivizing participation in conferences, ensuring the availability of technical references that promote deeper technical understanding, and occasionally bringing in outside experts (e.g., contractors) with deep technical knowledge in needed areas as funding permits.
- Give team members opportunities to perform other tasks, such as creating educational materials, conducting security awareness workshops, and performing research.
- Consider rotating staff members in and out of the incident response team, and participate in exchanges in which team members temporarily trade places with others (e.g., network administrators) to gain new technical skills.
- Maintain sufficient staffing so that team members can have uninterrupted time off work (e.g., vacations).
- Create a mentoring program to enable senior technical staff to help less experienced staff learn incident handling.
- Develop incident handling scenarios and have the team members discuss how they would handle them. Appendix A contains a set of scenarios and a list of questions to be used during scenario discussions.

Incident response team members should have other skills in addition to technical expertise. Teamwork skills are of fundamental importance because cooperation and coordination are necessary for successful incident response. Every team member should also have good communication skills. Speaking skills are important because the team will interact with a wide variety of people, and writing skills are important when team members are preparing advisories and procedures. Although not everyone within a team needs to have strong writing and speaking skills, at least a few people within every team should possess them so the team can represent itself well in front of others.

2.4.4 Dependencies within Organizations

It is important to identify other groups within the organization that may need to participate in incident handling so that their cooperation can be solicited before it is needed. Every incident response team relies on the expertise, judgment, and abilities of others, including:

- **Management.** Management establishes incident response policy, budget, and staffing. Ultimately, management is held responsible for coordinating incident response among various stakeholders, minimizing damage, and reporting to Congress, OMB, the General Accounting Office (GAO), and other parties.
- **Information Assurance.** Information security staff members may be needed during certain stages of incident handling (prevention, containment, eradication, and recovery)—for example, to alter network security controls (e.g., firewall rulesets).
- **IT Support.** IT technical experts (e.g., system and network administrators) not only have the needed skills to assist but also usually have the best understanding of the technology they manage on a daily basis. This understanding can ensure that the appropriate actions are taken for the affected system, such as whether to disconnect an attacked system.

- **Legal Department.** Legal experts should review incident response plans, policies, and procedures to ensure their compliance with law and Federal guidance, including the right to privacy. In addition, the guidance of the general counsel or legal department should be sought if there is reason to believe that an incident may have legal ramifications, including evidence collection, prosecution of a suspect, or a lawsuit, or if there may be a need for a memorandum of understanding (MOU) or other binding agreements involving liability limitations for information sharing.

- **Public Affairs and Media Relations.** Depending on the nature and impact of an incident, a need may exist to inform the media and, by extension, the public.

- **Human Resources.** If an employee is suspected of causing an incident, the human resources department may be involved—for example, in assisting with disciplinary proceedings.

- **Business Continuity Planning.** Organizations should ensure that incident response policies and procedures and business continuity processes are in sync. Computer security incidents undermine the business resilience of an organization. Business continuity planning professionals should be made aware of incidents and their impacts so they can fine-tune business impact assessments, risk assessments, and continuity of operations plans. Further, because business continuity planners have extensive expertise in minimizing operational disruption during severe circumstances, they may be valuable in planning responses to certain situations, such as denial of service (DoS) conditions.

- **Physical Security and Facilities Management.** Some computer security incidents occur through breaches of physical security or involve coordinated logical and physical attacks. The incident response team also may need access to facilities during incident handling—for example, to acquire a compromised workstation from a locked office.

2.5 Incident Response Team Services

The main focus of an incident response team is performing incident response, but it is fairly rare for a team to perform incident response only. The following are examples of other services a team might offer:

- **Intrusion Detection.** The first tier of an incident response team often assumes responsibility for intrusion detection.[17] The team generally benefits because it should be poised to analyze incidents more quickly and accurately, based on the knowledge it gains of intrusion detection technologies.

- **Advisory Distribution.** A team may issue advisories within the organization regarding new vulnerabilities and threats.[18] Automated methods should be used whenever appropriate to disseminate information; for example, the National Vulnerability Database (NVD) provides information via XML and RSS feeds when new vulnerabilities are added to it.[19] Advisories are often most necessary when new threats are emerging, such as a high-profile social or political event (e.g., celebrity wedding) that attackers are likely to leverage in their social engineering. Only one group within the organization should distribute computer security advisories to avoid duplicated effort and conflicting information.

- **Education and Awareness.** Education and awareness are resource multipliers—the more the users and technical staff know about detecting, reporting, and responding to incidents, the less drain there

---

17 See NIST SP 800-94, *Guide to Intrusion Detection and Prevention Systems (IDPS)* for more information on IDPS technologies. It is available at http://csrc nist.gov/publications/PubsSPs html#800-94.

18 Teams should word advisories so that they do not blame any person or organization for security issues. Teams should meet with legal advisors to discuss the possible need for a disclaimer in advisories, stating that the team and organization has no liability in regard to the accuracy of the advisory. This is most pertinent when advisories may be sent to contractors, vendors, and other nonemployees who are users of the organization's computing resources.

19 http://nvd nist.gov/

should be on the incident response team. This information can be communicated through many means: workshops, websites, newsletters, posters, and even stickers on monitors and laptops.

- **Information Sharing.** Incident response teams often participate in information sharing groups, such as ISACs or regional partnerships. Accordingly, incident response teams often manage the organization's incident information sharing efforts, such as aggregating information related to incidents and effectively sharing that information with other organizations, as well as ensuring that pertinent information is shared within the enterprise.

2.6 Recommendations

The key recommendations presented in this section for organizing a computer security incident handling capability are summarized below.

- **Establish a formal incident response capability.** Organizations should be prepared to respond quickly and effectively when computer security defenses are breached. FISMA requires Federal agencies to establish incident response capabilities.

- **Create an incident response policy.** The incident response policy is the foundation of the incident response program. It defines which events are considered incidents, establishes the organizational structure for incident response, defines roles and responsibilities, and lists the requirements for reporting incidents, among other items.

- **Develop an incident response plan based on the incident response policy.** The incident response plan provides a roadmap for implementing an incident response program based on the organization's policy. The plan indicates both short- and long-term goals for the program, including metrics for measuring the program. The incident response plan should also indicate how often incident handlers should be trained and the requirements for incident handlers.

- **Develop incident response procedures.** The incident response procedures provide detailed steps for responding to an incident. The procedures should cover all the phases of the incident response process. The procedures should be based on the incident response policy and plan.

- **Establish policies and procedures regarding incident-related information sharing.** The organization should communicate appropriate incident details with outside parties, such as the media, law enforcement agencies, and incident reporting organizations. The incident response team should discuss this with the organization's public affairs office, legal department, and management to establish policies and procedures regarding information sharing. The team should comply with existing organization policy on interacting with the media and other outside parties.

- **Provide pertinent information on incidents to the appropriate organization.** Federal civilian agencies are required to report incidents to US-CERT; other organizations can contact US-CERT and/or their ISAC. Reporting is beneficial because US-CERT and the ISACs use the reported data to provide information to the reporting parties regarding new threats and incident trends.

- **Consider the relevant factors when selecting an incident response team model.** Organizations should carefully weigh the advantages and disadvantages of each possible team structure model and staffing model in the context of the organization's needs and available resources.

- **Select people with appropriate skills for the incident response team.** The credibility and proficiency of the team depend to a large extent on the technical skills and critical thinking abilities of its members. Critical technical skills include system administration, network administration, programming, technical support, and intrusion detection. Teamwork and communications skills are also needed for effective incident handling. Necessary training should be provided to all team members.

- **Identify other groups within the organization that may need to participate in incident handling.** Every incident response team relies on the expertise, judgment, and abilities of other teams, including management, information assurance, IT support, legal, public affairs, and facilities management.

- **Determine which services the team should offer.** Although the main focus of the team is incident response, most teams perform additional functions. Examples include monitoring intrusion detection sensors, distributing security advisories, and educating users on security.

3. Handling an Incident

The incident response process has several phases. The initial phase involves establishing and training an incident response team, and acquiring the necessary tools and resources. During preparation, the organization also attempts to limit the number of incidents that will occur by selecting and implementing a set of controls based on the results of risk assessments. However, residual risk will inevitably persist after controls are implemented. Detection of security breaches is thus necessary to alert the organization whenever incidents occur. In keeping with the severity of the incident, the organization can mitigate the impact of the incident by containing it and ultimately recovering from it. During this phase, activity often cycles back to detection and analysis—for example, to see if additional hosts are infected by malware while eradicating a malware incident. After the incident is adequately handled, the organization issues a report that details the cause and cost of the incident and the steps the organization should take to prevent future incidents. This section describes the major phases of the incident response process—preparation, detection and analysis, containment, eradication and recovery, and post-incident activity—in detail. Figure 3-1 illustrates the incident response life cycle.

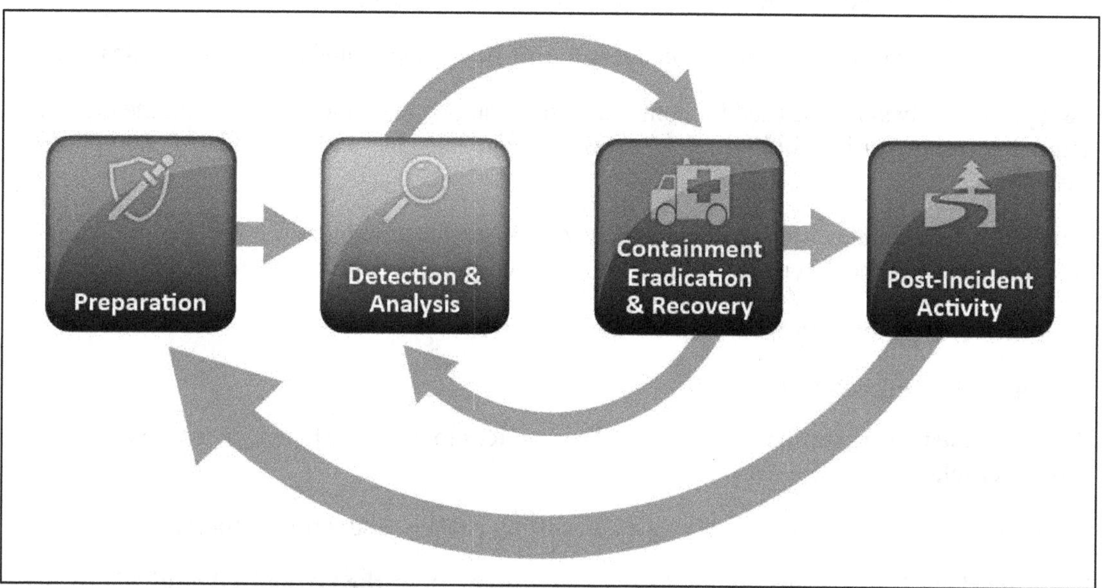

Figure 3-1. Incident Response Life Cycle

3.1 Preparation

Incident response methodologies typically emphasize preparation—not only establishing an incident response capability so that the organization is ready to respond to incidents, but also preventing incidents by ensuring that systems, networks, and applications are sufficiently secure. Although the incident response team is not typically responsible for incident prevention, it is fundamental to the success of incident response programs. This section provides basic advice on preparing to handle incidents and on preventing incidents.

3.1.1 Preparing to Handle Incidents

The lists below provide examples of tools and resources available that may be of value during incident handling. These lists are intended to be a starting point for discussions about which tools and resources an organization's incident handlers need. For example, smartphones are one way to have resilient emergency communication and coordination mechanisms. An organization should have multiple (separate and different) communication and coordination mechanisms in case of failure of one mechanism.

Incident Handler Communications and Facilities:

- **Contact information** for team members and others within and outside the organization (primary and backup contacts), such as law enforcement and other incident response teams; information may include phone numbers, email addresses, public encryption keys (in accordance with the encryption software described below), and instructions for verifying the contact's identity
- **On-call information** for other teams within the organization, including escalation information
- **Incident reporting mechanisms,** such as phone numbers, email addresses, online forms, and secure instant messaging systems that users can use to report suspected incidents; at least one mechanism should permit people to report incidents anonymously
- **Issue tracking system** for tracking incident information, status, etc.
- **Smartphones** to be carried by team members for off-hour support and onsite communications
- **Encryption software** to be used for communications among team members, within the organization and with external parties; for Federal agencies, software must use a FIPS-validated encryption algorithm[20]
- **War room** for central communication and coordination; if a permanent war room is not necessary or practical, the team should create a procedure for procuring a temporary war room when needed
- **Secure storage facility** for securing evidence and other sensitive materials

Incident Analysis Hardware and Software:

- **Digital forensic workstations[21] and/or backup devices** to create disk images, preserve log files, and save other relevant incident data
- **Laptops** for activities such as analyzing data, sniffing packets, and writing reports
- **Spare workstations, servers, and networking equipment, or the virtualized equivalents**, which may be used for many purposes, such as restoring backups and trying out malware
- **Blank removable media**
- **Portable printer** to print copies of log files and other evidence from non-networked systems
- **Packet sniffers and protocol analyzers** to capture and analyze network traffic
- **Digital forensic software** to analyze disk images
- **Removable media** with trusted versions of programs to be used to gather evidence from systems
- **Evidence gathering accessories**, including hard-bound notebooks, digital cameras, audio recorders, chain of custody forms, evidence storage bags and tags, and evidence tape, to preserve evidence for possible legal actions

---

20 FIPS 140-2, *Security Requirements for Cryptographic Modules*, http://csrc.nist.gov/publications/PubsFIPS.html.

21 A digital forensic workstation is specially designed to assist incident handlers in acquiring and analyzing data. These workstations typically contain a set of removable hard drives that can be used for evidence storage.

Incident Analysis Resources:

- **Port lists,** including commonly used ports and Trojan horse ports
- **Documentation** for OSs, applications, protocols, and intrusion detection and antivirus products
- **Network diagrams and lists of critical assets,** such as database servers
- **Current baselines** of expected network, system, and application activity
- **Cryptographic hashes** of critical files[22] to speed incident analysis, verification, and eradication

Incident Mitigation Software:

- **Access to images** of clean OS and application installations for restoration and recovery purposes

Many incident response teams create a *jump kit,* which is a portable case that contains materials that may be needed during an investigation. The jump kit should be ready to go at all times. Jump kits contain many of the same items listed in the bulleted lists above. For example, each jump kit typically includes a laptop, loaded with appropriate software (e.g., packet sniffers, digital forensics). Other important materials include backup devices, blank media, and basic networking equipment and cables. Because the purpose of having a jump kit is to facilitate faster responses, the team should avoid borrowing items from the jump kit.

Each incident handler should have access to at least two computing devices (e.g., laptops). One, such as the one from the jump kit, should be used to perform packet sniffing, malware analysis, and all other actions that risk contaminating the laptop that performs them. This laptop should be scrubbed and all software reinstalled before it is used for another incident. Note that because this laptop is special purpose, it is likely to use software other than the standard enterprise tools and configurations, and whenever possible the incident handlers should be allowed to specify basic technical requirements for these special-purpose investigative laptops. In addition to an investigative laptop, each incident handler should also have a standard laptop, smart phone, or other computing device for writing reports, reading email, and performing other duties unrelated to the hands-on incident analysis.

Exercises involving simulated incidents can also be very useful for preparing staff for incident handling; see NIST SP 800-84 for more information on exercises[23] and Appendix A for sample exercise scenarios.

3.1.2 Preventing Incidents

Keeping the number of incidents reasonably low is very important to protect the business processes of the organization. If security controls are insufficient, higher volumes of incidents may occur, overwhelming the incident response team. This can lead to slow and incomplete responses, which translate to a larger negative business impact (e.g., more extensive damage, longer periods of service and data unavailability).

It is outside the scope of this document to provide specific advice on securing networks, systems, and applications. Although incident response teams are generally not responsible for securing resources, they can be advocates of sound security practices. An incident response team may be able to identify problems that the organization is otherwise not aware of; the team can play a key role in risk assessment and training by identifying gaps. Other documents already provide advice on general security concepts and

---

22 The National Software Reference Library (NSRL) Project maintains records of hashes of various files, including operating system, application, and graphic image files. The hashes can be downloaded from http://www.nsrl.nist.gov/.

23 *Guide to Test, Training, and Exercise Programs for IT Plans and Capabilities,* http://csrc.nist.gov/publications/PubsSPs.html#800-84

operating system and application-specific guidelines.[24] The following text, however, provides a brief overview of some of the main recommended practices for securing networks, systems, and applications:

- **Risk Assessments.** Periodic risk assessments of systems and applications should determine what risks are posed by combinations of threats and vulnerabilities.[25] This should include understanding the applicable threats, including organization-specific threats. Each risk should be prioritized, and the risks can be mitigated, transferred, or accepted until a reasonable overall level of risk is reached. Another benefit of conducting risk assessments regularly is that critical resources are identified, allowing staff to emphasize monitoring and response activities for those resources.[26]
- **Host Security.** All hosts should be hardened appropriately using standard configurations. In addition to keeping each host properly patched, hosts should be configured to follow the principle of least privilege—granting users only the privileges necessary for performing their authorized tasks. Hosts should have auditing enabled and should log significant security-related events. The security of hosts and their configurations should be continuously monitored.[27] Many organizations use Security Content Automation Protocol (SCAP)[28] expressed operating system and application configuration checklists to assist in securing hosts consistently and effectively.[29]
- **Network Security.** The network perimeter should be configured to deny all activity that is not expressly permitted. This includes securing all connection points, such as virtual private networks (VPNs) and dedicated connections to other organizations.
- **Malware Prevention.** Software to detect and stop malware should be deployed throughout the organization. Malware protection should be deployed at the host level (e.g., server and workstation operating systems), the application server level (e.g., email server, web proxies), and the application client level (e.g., email clients, instant messaging clients).[30]
- **User Awareness and Training.** Users should be made aware of policies and procedures regarding appropriate use of networks, systems, and applications. Applicable lessons learned from previous incidents should also be shared with users so they can see how their actions could affect the organization. Improving user awareness regarding incidents should reduce the frequency of incidents. IT staff should be trained so that they can maintain their networks, systems, and applications in accordance with the organization's security standards.

---

24 http://csrc nist.gov/publications/PubsSPs.html provides links to the NIST Special Publications on computer security, which include documents on operating system and application security baselines.

25 Guidelines on risk assessment are available in NIST SP 800-30, *Guide for Conducting Risk Assessments*, at http://csrc nist.gov/publications/PubsSPs.html#800-30-Rev1.

26 Information on identifying critical resources is discussed in FIPS 199, *Standards for Security Categorization of Federal Information and Information Systems*, at http://csrc nist.gov/publications/PubsFIPS html.

27 For more information on continuous monitoring, see NIST SP 800-137, *Information Security Continuous Monitoring for Federal Information Systems and Organizations* (http://csrc.nist.gov/publications/PubsSPs html#800-137).

28 More information on SCAP is available from NIST SP 800-117 Revision 1, *Guide to Adopting and Using the Security Content Automation Protocol (SCAP) Version 1.2* (http://csrc nist.gov/publications/PubsSPs html#800-117).

29 NIST hosts a security checklists repository at http://checklists nist.gov/.

30 More information on malware prevention is available from NIST SP 800-83, *Guide to Malware Incident Prevention and Handling* (http://csrc nist.gov/publications/PubsSPs html#800-83).

3.2 Detection and Analysis

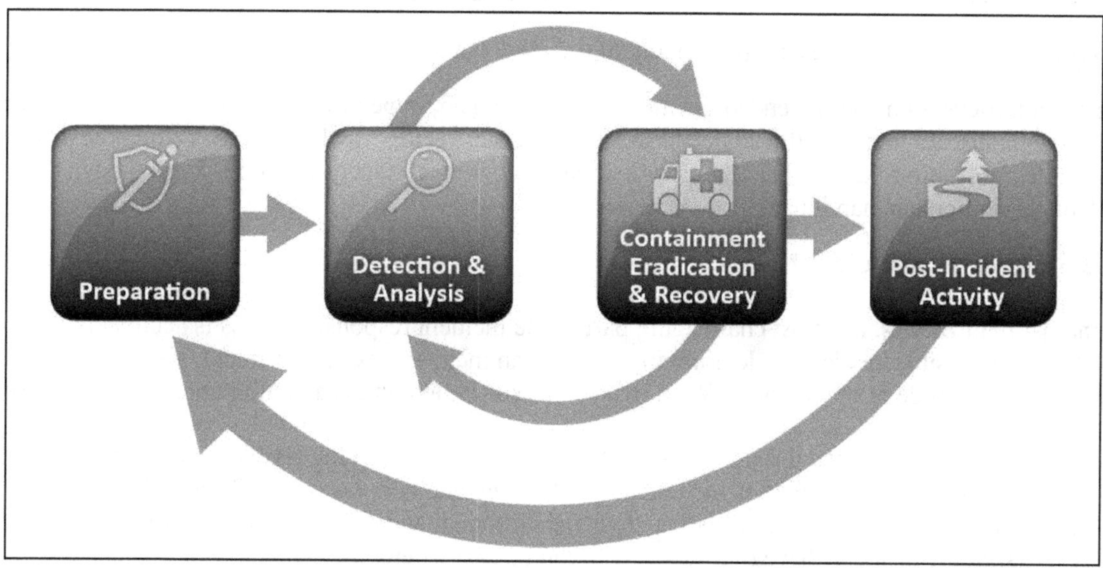

Figure 3-2. Incident Response Life Cycle (Detection and Analysis)

3.2.1 Attack Vectors

Incidents can occur in countless ways, so it is infeasible to develop step-by-step instructions for handling every incident. Organizations should be generally prepared to handle any incident but should focus on being prepared to handle incidents that use common attack vectors. Different types of incidents merit different response strategies. The attack vectors listed below are not intended to provide definitive classification for incidents; rather, they simply list common methods of attack, which can be used as a basis for defining more specific handling procedures.

- **External/Removable Media:** An attack executed from removable media or a peripheral device—for example, malicious code spreading onto a system from an infected USB flash drive.
- **Attrition:** An attack that employs brute force methods to compromise, degrade, or destroy systems, networks, or services (e.g., a DDoS intended to impair or deny access to a service or application; a brute force attack against an authentication mechanism, such as passwords, CAPTCHAS, or digital signatures).
- **Web:** An attack executed from a website or web-based application—for example, a cross-site scripting attack used to steal credentials or a redirect to a site that exploits a browser vulnerability and installs malware.
- **Email:** An attack executed via an email message or attachment—for example, exploit code disguised as an attached document or a link to a malicious website in the body of an email message.
- **Impersonation:** An attack involving replacement of something benign with something malicious—for example, spoofing, man in the middle attacks, rogue wireless access points, and SQL injection attacks all involve impersonation.
- **Improper Usage:** Any incident resulting from violation of an organization's acceptable usage policies by an authorized user, excluding the above categories; for example, a user installs file sharing software, leading to the loss of sensitive data; or a user performs illegal activities on a system.

- **Loss or Theft of Equipment:** The loss or theft of a computing device or media used by the organization, such as a laptop, smartphone, or authentication token.
- **Other:** An attack that does not fit into any of the other categories.

This section focuses on recommended practices for handling any type of incident. It is outside the scope of this publication to give specific advice based on the attack vectors; such guidelines would be provided in separate publications addressing other incident handling topics, such as NIST SP 800-83 on malware incident prevention and handling.

3.2.2 Signs of an Incident

For many organizations, the most challenging part of the incident response process is accurately detecting and assessing possible incidents—determining whether an incident has occurred and, if so, the type, extent, and magnitude of the problem. What makes this so challenging is a combination of three factors:

- Incidents may be detected through many different means, with varying levels of detail and fidelity. Automated detection capabilities include network-based and host-based IDPSs, antivirus software, and log analyzers. Incidents may also be detected through manual means, such as problems reported by users. Some incidents have overt signs that can be easily detected, whereas others are almost impossible to detect.
- The volume of potential signs of incidents is typically high—for example, it is not uncommon for an organization to receive thousands or even millions of intrusion detection sensor alerts per day. (See Section 3.2.4 for information on analyzing such alerts.)
- Deep, specialized technical knowledge and extensive experience are necessary for proper and efficient analysis of incident-related data.

Signs of an incident fall into one of two categories: precursors and indicators. A *precursor* is a sign that an incident may occur in the future. An *indicator* is a sign that an incident may have occurred or may be occurring now.

Most attacks do not have any identifiable or detectable precursors from the target's perspective. If precursors are detected, the organization may have an opportunity to prevent the incident by altering its security posture to save a target from attack. At a minimum, the organization could monitor activity involving the target more closely. Examples of precursors are:

- Web server log entries that show the usage of a vulnerability scanner
- An announcement of a new exploit that targets a vulnerability of the organization's mail server
- A threat from a group stating that the group will attack the organization.

While precursors are relatively rare, indicators are all too common. Too many types of indicators exist to exhaustively list them, but some examples are listed below:

- A network intrusion detection sensor alerts when a buffer overflow attempt occurs against a database server.
- Antivirus software alerts when it detects that a host is infected with malware.
- A system administrator sees a filename with unusual characters.
- A host records an auditing configuration change in its log.

- An application logs multiple failed login attempts from an unfamiliar remote system.
- An email administrator sees a large number of bounced emails with suspicious content.
- A network administrator notices an unusual deviation from typical network traffic flows.

3.2.3 Sources of Precursors and Indicators

Precursors and indicators are identified using many different sources, with the most common being computer security software alerts, logs, publicly available information, and people. Table 3-2 lists common sources of precursors and indicators for each category.

Table 3-1. Common Sources of Precursors and Indicators

Source	Description
	Alerts
IDPSs	IDPS products identify suspicious events and record pertinent data regarding them, including the date and time the attack was detected, the type of attack, the source and destination IP addresses, and the username (if applicable and known). Most IDPS products use attack signatures to identify malicious activity; the signatures must be kept up to date so that the newest attacks can be detected. IDPS software often produces *false positives*—alerts that indicate malicious activity is occurring, when in fact there has been none. Analysts should manually validate IDPS alerts either by closely reviewing the recorded supporting data or by getting related data from other sources.[31]
SIEMs	Security Information and Event Management (SIEM) products are similar to IDPS products, but they generate alerts based on analysis of log data (see below).
Antivirus and antispam software	Antivirus software detects various forms of malware, generates alerts, and prevents the malware from infecting hosts. Current antivirus products are effective at stopping many instances of malware if their signatures are kept up to date. Antispam software is used to detect spam and prevent it from reaching users' mailboxes. Spam may contain malware, phishing attacks, and other malicious content, so alerts from antispam software may indicate attack attempts.
File integrity checking software	File integrity checking software can detect changes made to important files during incidents. It uses a hashing algorithm to obtain a cryptographic checksum for each designated file. If the file is altered and the checksum is recalculated, an extremely high probability exists that the new checksum will not match the old checksum. By regularly recalculating checksums and comparing them with previous values, changes to files can be detected.
Third-party monitoring services	Third parties offer a variety of subscription-based and free monitoring services. An example is fraud detection services that will notify an organization if its IP addresses, domain names, etc. are associated with current incident activity involving other organizations. There are also free real-time blacklists with similar information. Another example of a third-party monitoring service is a CSIRC notification list; these lists are often available only to other incident response teams.
	Logs
Operating system, service and application logs	Logs from operating systems, services, and applications (particularly audit-related data) are frequently of great value when an incident occurs, such as recording which accounts were accessed and what actions were performed. Organizations should require a baseline level of logging on all systems and a higher baseline level on critical systems. Logs can be used for analysis by correlating event information. Depending on the event information, an alert can be generated to indicate an incident. Section 3.2.4 discusses the value of centralized logging.
Network device logs	Logs from network devices such as firewalls and routers are not typically a primary source of precursors or indicators. Although these devices are usually configured to log blocked connection attempts, they provide little information about the nature of the activity. Still, they can be valuable in identifying network trends and in correlating events detected by other devices.

[31] See NIST SP 800-94, *Guide to Intrusion Detection and Prevention Systems,* for additional information on IDPS products. It is available at http://csrc.nist.gov/publications/PubsSPs html#800-94.

Source	Description
Network flows	A network flow is a particular communication session occurring between hosts. Routers and other networking devices can provide network flow information, which can be used to find anomalous network activity caused by malware, data exfiltration, and other malicious acts. There are many standards for flow data formats, including NetFlow, sFlow, and IPFIX.
Publicly Available Information	
Information on new vulnerabilities and exploits	Keeping up with new vulnerabilities and exploits can prevent some incidents from occurring and assist in detecting and analyzing new attacks. The National Vulnerability Database (NVD) contains information on vulnerabilities.[32] Organizations such as US-CERT[33] and CERT®/CC periodically provide threat update information through briefings, web postings, and mailing lists.
People	
People from within the organization	Users, system administrators, network administrators, security staff, and others from within the organization may report signs of incidents. It is important to validate all such reports. One approach is to ask people who provide such information how confident they are of the accuracy of the information. Recording this estimate along with the information provided can help considerably during incident analysis, particularly when conflicting data is discovered.
People from other organizations	Reports of incidents that originate externally should be taken seriously. For example, the organization might be contacted by a party claiming a system at the organization is attacking its systems. External users may also report other indicators, such as a defaced web page or an unavailable service. Other incident response teams also may report incidents. It is important to have mechanisms in place for external parties to report indicators and for trained staff to monitor those mechanisms carefully; this may be as simple as setting up a phone number and email address, configured to forward messages to the help desk.

3.2.4 Incident Analysis

Incident detection and analysis would be easy if every precursor or indicator were guaranteed to be accurate; unfortunately, this is not the case. For example, user-provided indicators such as a complaint of a server being unavailable are often incorrect. Intrusion detection systems may produce false positives—incorrect indicators. These examples demonstrate what makes incident detection and analysis so difficult: each indicator ideally should be evaluated to determine if it is legitimate. Making matters worse, the total number of indicators may be thousands or millions a day. Finding the real security incidents that occurred out of all the indicators can be a daunting task.

Even if an indicator is accurate, it does not necessarily mean that an incident has occurred. Some indicators, such as a server crash or modification of critical files, could happen for several reasons other than a security incident, including human error. Given the occurrence of indicators, however, it is reasonable to suspect that an incident might be occurring and to act accordingly. Determining whether a particular event is actually an incident is sometimes a matter of judgment. It may be necessary to collaborate with other technical and information security personnel to make a decision. In many instances, a situation should be handled the same way regardless of whether it is security related. For example, if an organization is losing Internet connectivity every 12 hours and no one knows the cause, the staff would want to resolve the problem just as quickly and would use the same resources to diagnose the problem, regardless of its cause.

Some incidents are easy to detect, such as an obviously defaced web page. However, many incidents are not associated with such clear symptoms. Small signs such as one change in one system configuration file may be the only indicators that an incident has occurred. In incident handling, detection may be the most difficult task. Incident handlers are responsible for analyzing ambiguous, contradictory, and incomplete symptoms to determine what has happened. Although technical solutions exist that can make detection

32 http://nvd.nist.gov/
33 http://www.us-cert.gov/cas/signup.html

easier, the best remedy is to build a team of highly experienced and proficient staff members who can analyze the precursors and indicators effectively and efficiently and take appropriate actions. Without a well-trained and capable staff, incident detection and analysis will be conducted inefficiently, and costly mistakes will be made.

The incident response team should work quickly to analyze and validate each incident, following a pre-defined process and documenting each step taken. When the team believes that an incident has occurred, the team should rapidly perform an initial analysis to determine the incident's scope, such as which networks, systems, or applications are affected; who or what originated the incident; and how the incident is occurring (e.g., what tools or attack methods are being used, what vulnerabilities are being exploited). The initial analysis should provide enough information for the team to prioritize subsequent activities, such as containment of the incident and deeper analysis of the effects of the incident.

Performing the initial analysis and validation is challenging. The following are recommendations for making incident analysis easier and more effective:

- **Profile Networks and Systems.** *Profiling* is measuring the characteristics of expected activity so that changes to it can be more easily identified. Examples of profiling are running file integrity checking software on hosts to derive checksums for critical files and monitoring network bandwidth usage to determine what the average and peak usage levels are on various days and times. In practice, it is difficult to detect incidents accurately using most profiling techniques; organizations should use profiling as one of several detection and analysis techniques.

- **Understand Normal Behaviors.** Incident response team members should study networks, systems, and applications to understand what their normal behavior is so that abnormal behavior can be recognized more easily. No incident handler will have a comprehensive knowledge of all behavior throughout the environment, but handlers should know which experts could fill in the gaps. One way to gain this knowledge is through reviewing log entries and security alerts. This may be tedious if filtering is not used to condense the logs to a reasonable size. As handlers become more familiar with the logs and alerts, they should be able to focus on unexplained entries, which are usually more important to investigate. Conducting frequent log reviews should keep the knowledge fresh, and the analyst should be able to notice trends and changes over time. The reviews also give the analyst an indication of the reliability of each source.

- **Create a Log Retention Policy.** Information regarding an incident may be recorded in several places, such as firewall, IDPS, and application logs. Creating and implementing a log retention policy that specifies how long log data should be maintained may be extremely helpful in analysis because older log entries may show reconnaissance activity or previous instances of similar attacks. Another reason for retaining logs is that incidents may not be discovered until days, weeks, or even months later. The length of time to maintain log data is dependent on several factors, including the organization's data retention policies and the volume of data. See NIST SP 800-92, *Guide to Computer Security Log Management* for additional recommendations related to logging.[34]

- **Perform Event Correlation.** Evidence of an incident may be captured in several logs that each contain different types of data—a firewall log may have the source IP address that was used, whereas an application log may contain a username. A network IDPS may detect that an attack was launched against a particular host, but it may not know if the attack was successful. The analyst may need to examine the host's logs to determine that information. Correlating events among multiple indicator sources can be invaluable in validating whether a particular incident occurred.

[34] http://csrc nist.gov/publications/PubsSPs.html#800-92

- **Keep All Host Clocks Synchronized.** Protocols such as the Network Time Protocol (NTP) synchronize clocks among hosts.[35] Event correlation will be more complicated if the devices reporting events have inconsistent clock settings. From an evidentiary standpoint, it is preferable to have consistent timestamps in logs—for example, to have three logs that show an attack occurred at 12:07:01 a.m., rather than logs that list the attack as occurring at 12:07:01, 12:10:35, and 11:07:06.

- **Maintain and Use a Knowledge Base of Information.** The knowledge base should include information that handlers need for referencing quickly during incident analysis. Although it is possible to build a knowledge base with a complex structure, a simple approach can be effective. Text documents, spreadsheets, and relatively simple databases provide effective, flexible, and searchable mechanisms for sharing data among team members. The knowledge base should also contain a variety of information, including explanations of the significance and validity of precursors and indicators, such as IDPS alerts, operating system log entries, and application error codes.

- **Use Internet Search Engines for Research.** Internet search engines can help analysts find information on unusual activity. For example, an analyst may see some unusual connection attempts targeting TCP port 22912. Performing a search on the terms "TCP," "port," and "22912" may return some hits that contain logs of similar activity or even an explanation of the significance of the port number. Note that separate workstations should be used for research to minimize the risk to the organization from conducting these searches.

- **Run Packet Sniffers to Collect Additional Data.** Sometimes the indicators do not record enough detail to permit the handler to understand what is occurring. If an incident is occurring over a network, the fastest way to collect the necessary data may be to have a packet sniffer capture network traffic. Configuring the sniffer to record traffic that matches specified criteria should keep the volume of data manageable and minimize the inadvertent capture of other information. Because of privacy concerns, some organizations may require incident handlers to request and receive permission before using packet sniffers.

- **Filter the Data.** There is simply not enough time to review and analyze all the indicators; at minimum the most suspicious activity should be investigated. One effective strategy is to filter out categories of indicators that tend to be insignificant. Another filtering strategy is to show only the categories of indicators that are of the highest significance; however, this approach carries substantial risk because new malicious activity may not fall into one of the chosen indicator categories.

- **Seek Assistance from Others.** Occasionally, the team will be unable to determine the full cause and nature of an incident. If the team lacks sufficient information to contain and eradicate the incident, then it should consult with internal resources (e.g., information security staff) and external resources (e.g., US-CERT, other CSIRTs, contractors with incident response expertise). It is important to accurately determine the cause of each incident so that it can be fully contained and the exploited vulnerabilities can be mitigated to prevent similar incidents from occurring.

3.2.5 Incident Documentation

An incident response team that suspects that an incident has occurred should immediately start recording all facts regarding the incident.[36] A logbook is an effective and simple medium for this,[37] but laptops,

---

35 More information on NTP is available at http://www.ntp.org/.

36 Incident handlers should log only the facts regarding the incident, not personal opinions or conclusions. Subjective material should be presented in incident reports, not recorded as evidence.

37 If a logbook is used, it is preferable that the logbook is bound and that the incident handlers number the pages, write in ink, and leave the logbook intact (i.e., do not rip out any pages).

audio recorders, and digital cameras can also serve this purpose.[38] Documenting system events, conversations, and observed changes in files can lead to a more efficient, more systematic, and less error-prone handling of the problem. Every step taken from the time the incident was detected to its final resolution should be documented and timestamped. Every document regarding the incident should be dated and signed by the incident handler. Information of this nature can also be used as evidence in a court of law if legal prosecution is pursued. Whenever possible, handlers should work in teams of at least two: one person can record and log events while the other person performs the technical tasks. Section 3.3.2 presents more information about evidence.[39]

The incident response team should maintain records about the status of incidents, along with other pertinent information.[40] Using an application or a database, such as an issue tracking system, helps ensure that incidents are handled and resolved in a timely manner. The issue tracking system should contain information on the following:

- The current status of the incident (new, in progress, forwarded for investigation, resolved, etc.)
- A summary of the incident
- Indicators related to the incident
- Other incidents related to this incident
- Actions taken by all incident handlers on this incident
- Chain of custody, if applicable
- Impact assessments related to the incident
- Contact information for other involved parties (e.g., system owners, system administrators)
- A list of evidence gathered during the incident investigation
- Comments from incident handlers
- Next steps to be taken (e.g., rebuild the host, upgrade an application).[41]

The incident response team should safeguard incident data and restrict access to it because it often contains sensitive information—for example, data on exploited vulnerabilities, recent security breaches, and users that may have performed inappropriate actions. For example, only authorized personnel should have access to the incident database. Incident communications (e.g., emails) and documents should be encrypted or otherwise protected so that only authorized personnel can read them.

---

38 Consider the admissibility of evidence collected with a device before using it. For example, any devices that are potential sources of evidence should not themselves be used to record other evidence.

39 NIST SP 800-86, *Guide to Integrating Forensic Techniques Into Incident Response,* provides detailed information on establishing a forensic capability, including the development of policies and procedures.

40 Appendix B contains a suggested list of data elements to collect when incidents are reported. Also, the CERT®/CC document *State of the Practice of Computer Security Incident Response Teams (CSIRTs)* provides several sample incident reporting forms. The document is available at http://www.cert.org/archive/pdf/03tr001.pdf.

41 The Trans-European Research and Education Networking Association (TERENA) has developed RFC 3067, *TERENA's Incident Object Description and Exchange Format Requirements* (http://www.ietf.org/rfc/rfc3067.txt). The document provides recommendations for what information should be collected for each incident. The IETF Extended Incident Handling (inch) Working Group (http://www.cert.org/ietf/inch/inch.html) created an RFC that expands on TERENA's work—RFC 5070, *Incident Object Description Exchange Format* (http://www.ietf.org/rfc/rfc5070.txt).

3.2.6 Incident Prioritization

Prioritizing the handling of the incident is perhaps the most critical decision point in the incident handling process. Incidents should not be handled on a first-come, first-served basis as a result of resource limitations. Instead, handling should be prioritized based on the relevant factors, such as the following:

- **Functional Impact of the Incident.** Incidents targeting IT systems typically impact the business functionality that those systems provide, resulting in some type of negative impact to the users of those systems. Incident handlers should consider how the incident will impact the existing functionality of the affected systems. Incident handlers should consider not only the current functional impact of the incident, but also the likely future functional impact of the incident if it is not immediately contained.

- **Information Impact of the Incident.** Incidents may affect the confidentiality, integrity, and availability of the organization's information. For example, a malicious agent may exfiltrate sensitive information. Incident handlers should consider how this information exfiltration will impact the organization's overall mission. An incident that results in the exfiltration of sensitive information may also affect other organizations if any of the data pertained to a partner organization.

- **Recoverability from the Incident.** The size of the incident and the type of resources it affects will determine the amount of time and resources that must be spent on recovering from that incident. In some instances it is not possible to recover from an incident (e.g., if the confidentiality of sensitive information has been compromised) and it would not make sense to spend limited resources on an elongated incident handling cycle, unless that effort was directed at ensuring that a similar incident did not occur in the future. In other cases, an incident may require far more resources to handle than what an organization has available. Incident handlers should consider the effort necessary to actually recover from an incident and carefully weigh that against the value the recovery effort will create and any requirements related to incident handling.

Combining the functional impact to the organization's systems and the impact to the organization's information determines the business impact of the incident—for example, a distributed denial of service attack against a public web server may temporarily reduce the functionality for users attempting to access the server, whereas unauthorized root-level access to a public web server may result in the exfiltration of personally identifiable information (PII), which could have a long-lasting impact on the organization's reputation.

The recoverability from the incident determines the possible responses that the team may take when handling the incident. An incident with a high functional impact and low effort to recover from is an ideal candidate for immediate action from the team. However, some incidents may not have smooth recovery paths and may need to be queued for a more strategic-level response—for example, an incident that results in an attacker exfiltrating and publicly posting gigabytes of sensitive data has no easy recovery path since the data is already exposed; in this case the team may transfer part of the responsibility for handling the data exfiltration incident to a more strategic-level team that develops strategy for preventing future breaches and creates an outreach plan for alerting those individuals or organizations whose data was exfiltrated. The team should prioritize the response to each incident based on its estimate of the business impact caused by the incident and the estimated efforts required to recover from the incident.

An organization can best quantify the effect of its own incidents because of its situational awareness. Table 3-2 provides examples of functional impact categories that an organization might use for rating its own incidents. Rating incidents can be helpful in prioritizing limited resources.

Table 3-2. Functional Impact Categories

Category	Definition
None	No effect to the organization's ability to provide all services to all users
Low	Minimal effect; the organization can still provide all critical services to all users but has lost efficiency
Medium	Organization has lost the ability to provide a critical service to a subset of system users
High	Organization is no longer able to provide some critical services to any users

Table 3-3 provides examples of possible information impact categories that describe the extent of information compromise that occurred during the incident. In this table, with the exception of the 'None' value, the categories are not mutually exclusive and the organization could choose more than one.

Table 3-3. Information Impact Categories

Category	Definition
None	No information was exfiltrated, changed, deleted, or otherwise compromised
Privacy Breach	Sensitive personally identifiable information (PII) of taxpayers, employees, beneficiaries, etc. was accessed or exfiltrated
Proprietary Breach	Unclassified proprietary information, such as protected critical infrastructure information (PCII), was accessed or exfiltrated
Integrity Loss	Sensitive or proprietary information was changed or deleted

Table 3-4 shows examples of recoverability effort categories that reflect the level of and type of resources required to recover from the incident.

Table 3-4. Recoverability Effort Categories

Category	Definition
Regular	Time to recovery is predictable with existing resources
Supplemented	Time to recovery is predictable with additional resources
Extended	Time to recovery is unpredictable; additional resources and outside help are needed
Not Recoverable	Recovery from the incident is not possible (e.g., sensitive data exfiltrated and posted publicly); launch investigation

Organizations should also establish an escalation process for those instances when the team does not respond to an incident within the designated time. This can happen for many reasons: for example, cell phones may fail or people may have personal emergencies. The escalation process should state how long a person should wait for a response and what to do if no response occurs. Generally, the first step is to duplicate the initial contact. After waiting for a brief time—perhaps 15 minutes—the caller should escalate the incident to a higher level, such as the incident response team manager. If that person does not respond within a certain time, then the incident should be escalated again to a higher level of management. This process should be repeated until someone responds.

3.2.7 Incident Notification

When an incident is analyzed and prioritized, the incident response team needs to notify the appropriate individuals so that all who need to be involved will play their roles. Incident response policies should include provisions concerning incident reporting—at a minimum, what must be reported to whom and at what times (e.g., initial notification, regular status updates). The exact reporting requirements vary among organizations, but parties that are typically notified include:

- CIO
- Head of information security
- Local information security officer
- Other incident response teams within the organization
- External incident response teams (if appropriate)
- System owner
- Human resources (for cases involving employees, such as harassment through email)
- Public affairs (for incidents that may generate publicity)
- Legal department (for incidents with potential legal ramifications)
- US-CERT (required for Federal agencies and systems operated on behalf of the Federal government; see Section 2.3.4.3)
- Law enforcement (if appropriate)

During incident handling, the team may need to provide status updates to certain parties, even in some cases the entire organization. The team should plan and prepare several communication methods, including out-of-band methods (e.g., in person, paper), and select the methods that are appropriate for a particular incident. Possible communication methods include:

- Email
- Website (internal, external, or portal)
- Telephone calls
- In person (e.g., daily briefings)
- Voice mailbox greeting (e.g., set up a separate voice mailbox for incident updates, and update the greeting message to reflect the current incident status; use the help desk's voice mail greeting)
- Paper (e.g., post notices on bulletin boards and doors, hand out notices at all entrance points).

3.3 Containment, Eradication, and Recovery

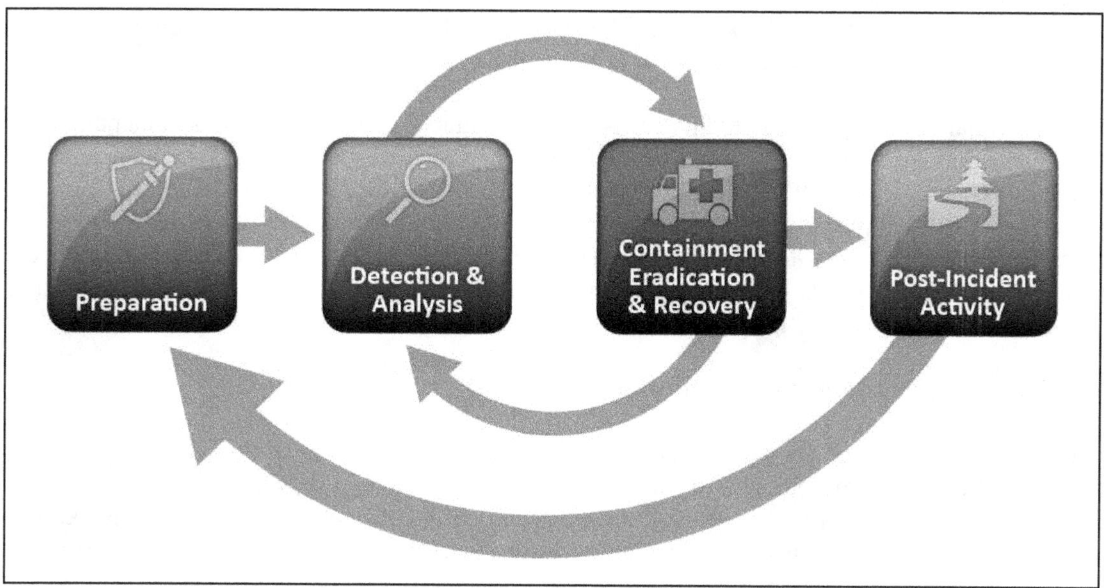

Figure 3-3. Incident Response Life Cycle (Containment, Eradication, and Recovery)

3.3.1 Choosing a Containment Strategy

Containment is important before an incident overwhelms resources or increases damage. Most incidents require containment, so that is an important consideration early in the course of handling each incident. Containment provides time for developing a tailored remediation strategy. An essential part of containment is decision-making (e.g., shut down a system, disconnect it from a network, disable certain functions). Such decisions are much easier to make if there are predetermined strategies and procedures for containing the incident. Organizations should define acceptable risks in dealing with incidents and develop strategies accordingly.

Containment strategies vary based on the type of incident. For example, the strategy for containing an email-borne malware infection is quite different from that of a network-based DDoS attack. Organizations should create separate containment strategies for each major incident type, with criteria documented clearly to facilitate decision-making. Criteria for determining the appropriate strategy include:

- Potential damage to and theft of resources
- Need for evidence preservation
- Service availability (e.g., network connectivity, services provided to external parties)
- Time and resources needed to implement the strategy
- Effectiveness of the strategy (e.g., partial containment, full containment)
- Duration of the solution (e.g., emergency workaround to be removed in four hours, temporary workaround to be removed in two weeks, permanent solution).

In certain cases, some organizations redirect the attacker to a sandbox (a form of containment) so that they can monitor the attacker's activity, usually to gather additional evidence. The incident response team should discuss this strategy with its legal department to determine if it is feasible. Ways of monitoring an attacker's activity other than sandboxing should not be used; if an organization knows that a system has been compromised and allows the compromise to continue, it may be liable if the attacker uses the compromised system to attack other systems. The delayed containment strategy is dangerous because an attacker could escalate unauthorized access or compromise other systems.

Another potential issue regarding containment is that some attacks may cause additional damage when they are contained. For example, a compromised host may run a malicious process that pings another host periodically. When the incident handler attempts to contain the incident by disconnecting the compromised host from the network, the subsequent pings will fail. As a result of the failure, the malicious process may overwrite or encrypt all the data on the host's hard drive. Handlers should not assume that just because a host has been disconnected from the network, further damage to the host has been prevented.

3.3.2 Evidence Gathering and Handling

Although the primary reason for gathering evidence during an incident is to resolve the incident, it may also be needed for legal proceedings.[42] In such cases, it is important to clearly document how all evidence, including compromised systems, has been preserved.[43] Evidence should be collected according to procedures that meet all applicable laws and regulations that have been developed from previous discussions with legal staff and appropriate law enforcement agencies so that any evidence can be admissible in court.[44] In addition, evidence should be accounted for at all times; whenever evidence is transferred from person to person, chain of custody forms should detail the transfer and include each party's signature. A detailed log should be kept for all evidence, including the following:

- Identifying information (e.g., the location, serial number, model number, hostname, media access control (MAC) addresses, and IP addresses of a computer)
- Name, title, and phone number of each individual who collected or handled the evidence during the investigation
- Time and date (including time zone) of each occurrence of evidence handling
- Locations where the evidence was stored.

Collecting evidence from computing resources presents some challenges. It is generally desirable to acquire evidence from a system of interest as soon as one suspects that an incident may have occurred. Many incidents cause a dynamic chain of events to occur; an initial system snapshot may do more good in identifying the problem and its source than most other actions that can be taken at this stage. From an evidentiary standpoint, it is much better to get a snapshot of the system as-is rather than doing so after incident handlers, system administrators, and others have inadvertently altered the state of the machine during the investigation. Users and system administrators should be made aware of the steps that they should take to preserve evidence. See NIST SP 800-86, *Guide to Integrating Forensic Techniques into Incident Response*, for additional information on preserving evidence.

---

42 NIST SP 800-86, *Guide to Integrating Forensic Techniques into Incident Response,* provides detailed information on establishing a forensic capability. It focuses on forensic techniques for PCs, but much of the material is applicable to other systems. The document can be found at http://csrc nist.gov/publications/PubsSPs html#800-86.

43 Evidence gathering and handling is not typically performed for every incident that occurs—for example, most malware incidents do not merit evidence acquisition. In many organizations, digital forensics is not needed for most incidents.

44 *Searching and Seizing Computers and Obtaining Electronic Evidence in Criminal Investigations*, from the Computer Crime and Intellectual Property Section (CCIPS) of the Department of Justice, provides legal guidance on evidence gathering. The document is available at http://www.cybercrime.gov/ssmanual/index html.

3.3.3 Identifying the Attacking Hosts

During incident handling, system owners and others sometimes want to or need to identify the attacking host or hosts. Although this information can be important, incident handlers should generally stay focused on containment, eradication, and recovery. Identifying an attacking host can be a time-consuming and futile process that can prevent a team from achieving its primary goal—minimizing the business impact. The following items describe the most commonly performed activities for attacking host identification:

- **Validating the Attacking Host's IP Address.** New incident handlers often focus on the attacking host's IP address. The handler may attempt to validate that the address was not spoofed by verifying connectivity to it; however, this simply indicates that a host at that address does or does not respond to the requests. A failure to respond does not mean the address is not real—for example, a host may be configured to ignore pings and traceroutes. Also, the attacker may have received a dynamic address that has already been reassigned to someone else.

- **Researching the Attacking Host through Search Engines.** Performing an Internet search using the apparent source IP address of an attack may lead to more information on the attack—for example, a mailing list message regarding a similar attack.

- **Using Incident Databases.** Several groups collect and consolidate incident data from various organizations into incident databases. This information sharing may take place in many forms, such as trackers and real-time blacklists. The organization can also check its own knowledge base or issue tracking system for related activity.

- **Monitoring Possible Attacker Communication Channels.** Incident handlers can monitor communication channels that may be used by an attacking host. For example, many bots use IRC as their primary means of communication. Also, attackers may congregate on certain IRC channels to brag about their compromises and share information. However, incident handlers should treat any such information that they acquire only as a potential lead, not as fact.

3.3.4 Eradication and Recovery

After an incident has been contained, eradication may be necessary to eliminate components of the incident, such as deleting malware and disabling breached user accounts, as well as identifying and mitigating all vulnerabilities that were exploited. During eradication, it is important to identify all affected hosts within the organization so that they can be remediated. For some incidents, eradication is either not necessary or is performed during recovery.

In recovery, administrators restore systems to normal operation, confirm that the systems are functioning normally, and (if applicable) remediate vulnerabilities to prevent similar incidents. Recovery may involve such actions as restoring systems from clean backups, rebuilding systems from scratch, replacing compromised files with clean versions, installing patches, changing passwords, and tightening network perimeter security (e.g., firewall rulesets, boundary router access control lists). Higher levels of system logging or network monitoring are often part of the recovery process. Once a resource is successfully attacked, it is often attacked again, or other resources within the organization are attacked in a similar manner.

Eradication and recovery should be done in a phased approach so that remediation steps are prioritized. For large-scale incidents, recovery may take months; the intent of the early phases should be to increase the overall security with relatively quick (days to weeks) high value changes to prevent future incidents. The later phases should focus on longer-term changes (e.g., infrastructure changes) and ongoing work to keep the enterprise as secure as possible.

Because eradication and recovery actions are typically OS or application-specific, detailed recommendations and advice regarding them are outside the scope of this document.

3.4 Post-Incident Activity

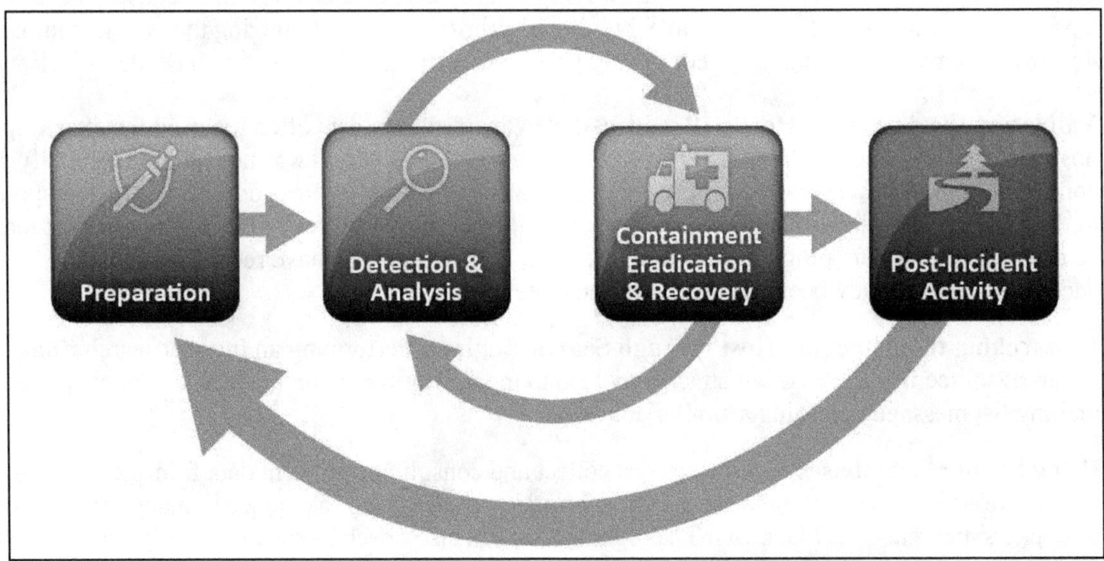

Figure 3-4. Incident Response Life Cycle (Post-Incident Activity)

3.4.1 Lessons Learned

One of the most important parts of incident response is also the most often omitted: learning and improving. Each incident response team should evolve to reflect new threats, improved technology, and lessons learned. Holding a "lessons learned" meeting with all involved parties after a major incident, and optionally periodically after lesser incidents as resources permit, can be extremely helpful in improving security measures and the incident handling process itself. Multiple incidents can be covered in a single lessons learned meeting. This meeting provides a chance to achieve closure with respect to an incident by reviewing what occurred, what was done to intervene, and how well intervention worked. The meeting should be held within several days of the end of the incident. Questions to be answered in the meeting include:

- Exactly what happened, and at what times?
- How well did staff and management perform in dealing with the incident? Were the documented procedures followed? Were they adequate?
- What information was needed sooner?
- Were any steps or actions taken that might have inhibited the recovery?
- What would the staff and management do differently the next time a similar incident occurs?
- How could information sharing with other organizations have been improved?
- What corrective actions can prevent similar incidents in the future?
- What precursors or indicators should be watched for in the future to detect similar incidents?

- What additional tools or resources are needed to detect, analyze, and mitigate future incidents?

Small incidents need limited post-incident analysis, with the exception of incidents performed through new attack methods that are of widespread concern and interest. After serious attacks have occurred, it is usually worthwhile to hold post-mortem meetings that cross team and organizational boundaries to provide a mechanism for information sharing. The primary consideration in holding such meetings is ensuring that the right people are involved. Not only is it important to invite people who have been involved in the incident that is being analyzed, but also it is wise to consider who should be invited for the purpose of facilitating future cooperation.

The success of such meetings also depends on the agenda. Collecting input about expectations and needs (including suggested topics to cover) from participants before the meeting increases the likelihood that the participants' needs will be met. In addition, establishing rules of order before or during the start of a meeting can minimize confusion and discord. Having one or more moderators who are skilled in group facilitation can yield a high payoff. Finally, it is also important to document the major points of agreement and action items and to communicate them to parties who could not attend the meeting.

Lessons learned meetings provide other benefits. Reports from these meetings are good material for training new team members by showing them how more experienced team members respond to incidents. Updating incident response policies and procedures is another important part of the lessons learned process. Post-mortem analysis of the way an incident was handled will often reveal a missing step or an inaccuracy in a procedure, providing impetus for change. Because of the changing nature of information technology and changes in personnel, the incident response team should review all related documentation and procedures for handling incidents at designated intervals.

Another important post-incident activity is creating a follow-up report for each incident, which can be quite valuable for future use. The report provides a reference that can be used to assist in handling similar incidents. Creating a formal chronology of events (including timestamped information such as log data from systems) is important for legal reasons, as is creating a monetary estimate of the amount of damage the incident caused. This estimate may become the basis for subsequent prosecution activity by entities such as the U.S. Attorney General's office. Follow-up reports should be kept for a period of time as specified in record retention policies.[45]

3.4.2 Using Collected Incident Data

Lessons learned activities should produce a set of objective and subjective data regarding each incident. Over time, the collected incident data should be useful in several capacities. The data, particularly the total hours of involvement and the cost, may be used to justify additional funding of the incident response team. A study of incident characteristics may indicate systemic security weaknesses and threats, as well as changes in incident trends. This data can be put back into the risk assessment process, ultimately leading to the selection and implementation of additional controls. Another good use of the data is measuring the success of the incident response team. If incident data is collected and stored properly, it should provide several measures of the success (or at least the activities) of the incident response team. Incident data can also be collected to determine if a change to incident response capabilities causes a corresponding change in the team's performance (e.g., improvements in efficiency, reductions in costs). Furthermore, organizations that are required to report incident information will need to collect the

---

45 General Records Schedule (GRS) 24, *Information Technology Operations and Management Records*, specifies that "computer security incident handling, reporting and follow-up records" should be destroyed "3 years after all necessary follow-up actions have been completed." GRS 24 is available from the National Archives and Records Administration at http://www.archives.gov/records-mgmt/grs/grs24.html.

necessary data to meet their requirements. See Section 4 for additional information on sharing incident data with other organizations.

Organizations should focus on collecting data that is actionable, rather than collecting data simply because it is available. For example, counting the number of precursor port scans that occur each week and producing a chart at the end of the year that shows port scans increased by eight percent is not very helpful and may be quite time-consuming. Absolute numbers are not informative—understanding how they represent threats to the business processes of the organization is what matters. Organizations should decide what incident data to collect based on reporting requirements and on the expected return on investment from the data (e.g., identifying a new threat and mitigating the related vulnerabilities before they can be exploited.) Possible metrics for incident-related data include:

- **Number of Incidents Handled.**[46] Handling more incidents is not necessarily better—for example, the number of incidents handled may decrease because of better network and host security controls, not because of negligence by the incident response team. The number of incidents handled is best taken as a measure of the relative amount of work that the incident response team had to perform, not as a measure of the quality of the team, unless it is considered in the context of other measures that collectively give an indication of work quality. It is more effective to produce separate incident counts for each incident category. Subcategories also can be used to provide more information. For example, a growing number of incidents performed by insiders could prompt stronger policy provisions concerning background investigations for personnel and misuse of computing resources and stronger security controls on internal networks (e.g., deploying intrusion detection software to more internal networks and hosts).
- **Time Per Incident.** For each incident, time can be measured in several ways:
  - Total amount of labor spent working on the incident
  - Elapsed time from the beginning of the incident to incident discovery, to the initial impact assessment, and to each stage of the incident handling process (e.g., containment, recovery)
  - How long it took the incident response team to respond to the initial report of the incident
  - How long it took to report the incident to management and, if necessary, appropriate external entities (e.g., US-CERT).
- **Objective Assessment of Each Incident.** The response to an incident that has been resolved can be analyzed to determine how effective it was. The following are examples of performing an objective assessment of an incident:
  - Reviewing logs, forms, reports, and other incident documentation for adherence to established incident response policies and procedures
  - Identifying which precursors and indicators of the incident were recorded to determine how effectively the incident was logged and identified
  - Determining if the incident caused damage before it was detected

---

46 Metrics such as the number of incidents handled are generally not of value in a comparison of multiple organizations because each organization is likely to have defined key terms differently. For example, most organizations define "incident" in terms of their own policies and practices, and what one organization considers a single incident may be considered multiple incidents by others. More specific metrics, such as the number of port scans, are also of little value in organizational comparisons. For example, it is highly unlikely that different security systems, such as network intrusion detection sensors, would all use the same criteria in labeling activity as a port scan.

  - Determining if the actual cause of the incident was identified, and identifying the vector of attack, the vulnerabilities exploited, and the characteristics of the targeted or victimized systems, networks, and applications
  - Determining if the incident is a recurrence of a previous incident
  - Calculating the estimated monetary damage from the incident (e.g., information and critical business processes negatively affected by the incident)
  - Measuring the difference between the initial impact assessment and the final impact assessment (see Section 3.2.6)
  - Identifying which measures, if any, could have prevented the incident.
- **Subjective Assessment of Each Incident.** Incident response team members may be asked to assess their own performance, as well as that of other team members and of the entire team. Another valuable source of input is the owner of a resource that was attacked, in order to determine if the owner thinks the incident was handled efficiently and if the outcome was satisfactory.

Besides using these metrics to measure the team's success, organizations may also find it useful to periodically audit their incident response programs. Audits will identify problems and deficiencies that can then be corrected. At a minimum, an incident response audit should evaluate the following items against applicable regulations, policies, and generally accepted practices:

- Incident response policies, plans, and procedures
- Tools and resources
- Team model and structure
- Incident handler training and education
- Incident documentation and reports
- The measures of success discussed earlier in this section.

3.4.3 Evidence Retention

Organizations should establish policy for how long evidence from an incident should be retained. Most organizations choose to retain all evidence for months or years after the incident ends. The following factors should be considered during the policy creation:

- **Prosecution.** If it is possible that the attacker will be prosecuted, evidence may need to be retained until all legal actions have been completed. In some cases, this may take several years. Furthermore, evidence that seems insignificant now may become more important in the future. For example, if an attacker is able to use knowledge gathered in one attack to perform a more severe attack later, evidence from the first attack may be key to explaining how the second attack was accomplished.
- **Data Retention.** Most organizations have data retention policies that state how long certain types of data may be kept. For example, an organization may state that email messages should be retained for only 180 days. If a disk image contains thousands of emails, the organization may not want the image to be kept for more than 180 days unless it is absolutely necessary. As discussed in Section 3.4.2, General Records Schedule (GRS) 24 specifies that incident handling records should be kept for three years.

- **Cost.** Original hardware (e.g., hard drives, compromised systems) that is stored as evidence, as well as hard drives and removable media that are used to hold disk images, are generally individually inexpensive. However, if an organization stores many such components for years, the cost can be substantial. The organization also must retain functional computers that can use the stored hardware and media.

3.5 Incident Handling Checklist

The checklist in Table 3-6 provides the major steps to be performed in the handling of an incident. Note that the actual steps performed may vary based on the type of incident and the nature of individual incidents. For example, if the handler knows exactly what has happened based on analysis of indicators (Step 1.1), there may be no need to perform Steps 1.2 or 1.3 to further research the activity. The checklist provides guidelines to handlers on the major steps that should be performed; it does not dictate the exact sequence of steps that should always be followed.

Table 3-5. Incident Handling Checklist

	Action	Completed
	Detection and Analysis	
1.	Determine whether an incident has occurred	
1.1	Analyze the precursors and indicators	
1.2	Look for correlating information	
1.3	Perform research (e.g., search engines, knowledge base)	
1.4	As soon as the handler believes an incident has occurred, begin documenting the investigation and gathering evidence	
2.	Prioritize handling the incident based on the relevant factors (functional impact, information impact, recoverability effort, etc.)	
3.	Report the incident to the appropriate internal personnel and external organizations	
	Containment, Eradication, and Recovery	
4.	Acquire, preserve, secure, and document evidence	
5.	Contain the incident	
6.	Eradicate the incident	
6.1	Identify and mitigate all vulnerabilities that were exploited	
6.2	Remove malware, inappropriate materials, and other components	
6.3	If more affected hosts are discovered (e.g., new malware infections), repeat the Detection and Analysis steps (1.1, 1.2) to identify all other affected hosts, then contain (5) and eradicate (6) the incident for them	
7.	Recover from the incident	
7.1	Return affected systems to an operationally ready state	
7.2	Confirm that the affected systems are functioning normally	
7.3	If necessary, implement additional monitoring to look for future related activity	
	Post-Incident Activity	
8.	Create a follow-up report	
9.	Hold a lessons learned meeting (mandatory for major incidents, optional otherwise)	

3.6 Recommendations

The key recommendations presented in this section for handling incidents are summarized below.

- **Acquire tools and resources that may be of value during incident handling.** The team will be more efficient at handling incidents if various tools and resources are already available to them. Examples include contact lists, encryption software, network diagrams, backup devices, digital forensic software, and port lists.
- **Prevent incidents from occurring by ensuring that networks, systems, and applications are sufficiently secure.** Preventing incidents is beneficial to the organization and also reduces the workload of the incident response team. Performing periodic risk assessments and reducing the identified risks to an acceptable level are effective in reducing the number of incidents. Awareness of security policies and procedures by users, IT staff, and management is also very important.
- **Identify precursors and indicators through alerts generated by several types of security software.** Intrusion detection and prevention systems, antivirus software, and file integrity checking software are valuable for detecting signs of incidents. Each type of software may detect incidents that the other types of software cannot, so the use of several types of computer security software is highly recommended. Third-party monitoring services can also be helpful.
- **Establish mechanisms for outside parties to report incidents.** Outside parties may want to report incidents to the organization—for example, they may believe that one of the organization's users is attacking them. Organizations should publish a phone number and email address that outside parties can use to report such incidents.
- **Require a baseline level of logging and auditing on all systems, and a higher baseline level on all critical systems.** Logs from operating systems, services, and applications frequently provide value during incident analysis, particularly if auditing was enabled. The logs can provide information such as which accounts were accessed and what actions were performed.
- **Profile networks and systems.** Profiling measures the characteristics of expected activity levels so that changes in patterns can be more easily identified. If the profiling process is automated, deviations from expected activity levels can be detected and reported to administrators quickly, leading to faster detection of incidents and operational issues.
- **Understand the normal behaviors of networks, systems, and applications.** Team members who understand normal behavior should be able to recognize abnormal behavior more easily. This knowledge can best be gained by reviewing log entries and security alerts; the handlers should become familiar with the typical data and can investigate the unusual entries to gain more knowledge.
- **Create a log retention policy.** Information regarding an incident may be recorded in several places. Creating and implementing a log retention policy that specifies how long log data should be maintained may be extremely helpful in analysis because older log entries may show reconnaissance activity or previous instances of similar attacks.
- **Perform event correlation.** Evidence of an incident may be captured in several logs. Correlating events among multiple sources can be invaluable in collecting all the available information for an incident and validating whether the incident occurred.
- **Keep all host clocks synchronized.** If the devices reporting events have inconsistent clock settings, event correlation will be more complicated. Clock discrepancies may also cause issues from an evidentiary standpoint.
- **Maintain and use a knowledge base of information.** Handlers need to reference information quickly during incident analysis; a centralized knowledge base provides a consistent, maintainable source of information. The knowledge base should include general information, such as data on precursors and indicators of previous incidents.

- **Start recording all information as soon as the team suspects that an incident has occurred.** Every step taken, from the time the incident was detected to its final resolution, should be documented and timestamped. Information of this nature can serve as evidence in a court of law if legal prosecution is pursued. Recording the steps performed can also lead to a more efficient, systematic, and less error-prone handling of the problem.
- **Safeguard incident data.** It often contains sensitive information regarding such things as vulnerabilities, security breaches, and users that may have performed inappropriate actions. The team should ensure that access to incident data is restricted properly, both logically and physically.
- **Prioritize handling of the incidents based on the relevant factors.** Because of resource limitations, incidents should not be handled on a first-come, first-served basis. Instead, organizations should establish written guidelines that outline how quickly the team must respond to the incident and what actions should be performed, based on relevant factors such as the functional and information impact of the incident, and the likely recoverability from the incident. This saves time for the incident handlers and provides a justification to management and system owners for their actions. Organizations should also establish an escalation process for those instances when the team does not respond to an incident within the designated time.
- **Include provisions regarding incident reporting in the organization's incident response policy.** Organizations should specify which incidents must be reported, when they must be reported, and to whom. The parties most commonly notified are the CIO, head of information security, local information security officer, other incident response teams within the organization, and system owners.
- **Establish strategies and procedures for containing incidents.** It is important to contain incidents quickly and effectively to limit their business impact. Organizations should define acceptable risks in containing incidents and develop strategies and procedures accordingly. Containment strategies should vary based on the type of incident.
- **Follow established procedures for evidence gathering and handling.** The team should clearly document how all evidence has been preserved. Evidence should be accounted for at all times. The team should meet with legal staff and law enforcement agencies to discuss evidence handling, then develop procedures based on those discussions.
- **Capture volatile data from systems as evidence.** This includes lists of network connections, processes, login sessions, open files, network interface configurations, and the contents of memory. Running carefully chosen commands from trusted media can collect the necessary information without damaging the system's evidence.
- **Obtain system snapshots through full forensic disk images, not file system backups.** Disk images should be made to sanitized write-protectable or write-once media. This process is superior to a file system backup for investigatory and evidentiary purposes. Imaging is also valuable in that it is much safer to analyze an image than it is to perform analysis on the original system because the analysis may inadvertently alter the original.
- **Hold lessons learned meetings after major incidents.** Lessons learned meetings are extremely helpful in improving security measures and the incident handling process itself.

4. Coordination and Information Sharing

The nature of contemporary threats and attacks makes it more important than ever for organizations to work together during incident response. Organizations should ensure that they effectively coordinate portions of their incident response activities with appropriate partners. The most important aspect of incident response coordination is information sharing, where different organizations share threat, attack, and vulnerability information with each other so that each organization's knowledge benefits the other. Incident information sharing is frequently mutually beneficial because the same threats and attacks often affect multiple organizations simultaneously.

As mentioned in Section 2, coordinating and sharing information with partner organizations can strengthen the organization's ability to effectively respond to IT incidents. For example, if an organization identifies some behavior on its network that seems suspicious and sends information about the event to a set of trusted partners, someone else in that network may have already seen similar behavior and be able to respond with additional details about the suspicious activity, including signatures, other indicators to look for, or suggested remediation actions. Collaboration with the trusted partner can enable an organization to respond to the incident more quickly and efficiently than an organization operating in isolation.

This increase in efficiency for standard incident response techniques is not the only incentive for cross-organization coordination and information sharing. Another incentive for information sharing is the ability to respond to incidents using techniques that may not be available to a single organization, especially if that organization is small to medium size. For example, a small organization that identifies a particularly complex instance of malware on its network may not have the in-house resources to fully analyze the malware and determine its effect on the system. In this case, the organization may be able to leverage a trusted information sharing network to effectively outsource the analysis of this malware to third party resources that have the adequate technical capabilities to perform the malware analysis.

This section of the document highlights coordination and information sharing. Section 4.1 presents an overview of incident response coordination and focuses on the need for cross-organization coordination to supplement organization incident response processes. Section 4.2 discusses techniques for information sharing across organizations, and Section 4.3 examines how to restrict what information is shared or not shared with other organizations.

4.1 Coordination

As discussed in Section 2.3.4, an organization may need to interact with several types of external organizations in the course of conducting incident response activities. Examples of these organizations include other incident response teams, law enforcement agencies, Internet service providers, and constituents and customers. An organization's incident response team should plan its incident coordination with those parties before incidents occur to ensure that all parties know their roles and that effective lines of communication are established. Figure 4-1 provides a sample view into an organization performing coordination at every phase of the incident response lifecycle, highlighting that coordination is valuable throughout the lifecycle.

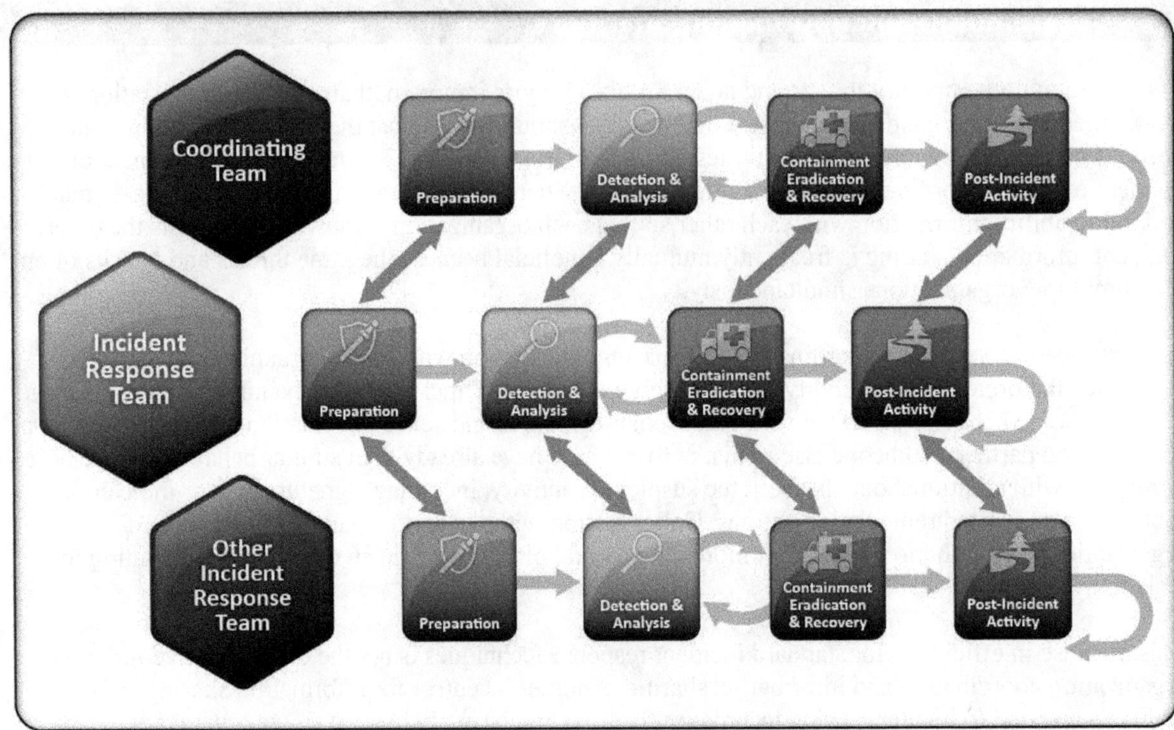

Figure 4-1. Incident Response Coordination

4.1.1 Coordination Relationships

An incident response team within an organization may participate in different types of coordination arrangements, depending on the type of organization with which it is coordinating. For example, the team members responsible for the technical details of incident response may coordinate with operational colleagues at partner organizations to share strategies for mitigating an attack spanning multiple organizations. Alternatively, during the same incident, the incident response team manager may coordinate with ISACs to satisfy necessary reporting requirements and seek advice and additional resources for successfully responding to the incident. Table 4-1 provides some examples of coordination relationships that may exist when collaborating with outside organizations.

Table 4-1. Coordination Relationships

Category	Definition	Information Shared
Team-to-team	Team-to-team relationships exist whenever technical incident responders in different organizations collaborate with their peers during any phase of the incident handling life cycle. The organizations participating in this type of relationship are usually peers without any authority over each other and choose to share information, pool resources, and reuse knowledge to solve problems common to both teams.	The information most frequently shared in team-to-team relationships is tactical and technical (e.g., technical indicators of compromise, suggested remediation actions) but may also include other types of information (plans, procedures, lessons learned) if conducted as part of the Preparation phase.
Team-to-coordinating team	Team-to-coordinating team relationships exist between an organizational incident response team and a separate organization that acts as a central point for coordinated incident response and management such as US-CERT or an ISAC. This type of relationship may include some degree of required reporting from the member organizations by the coordinating body, as well as the expectation that the coordinating team will disseminate timely and useful information to participating member organizations.	Teams and coordinating teams frequently share tactical, technical information as well as information regarding threats, vulnerabilities, and risks to the community served by the coordinating team. The coordinating team may also need specific impact information about incidents in order to help make decisions on where to focus its resources and attention.
Coordinating team-to-coordinating team	Relationships between multiple coordinating teams such as US-CERT and the ISACs exist to share information relating to cross-cutting incidents which may affect multiple communities. The coordinating teams act on behalf of their respective community member organizations to share information on the nature and scope of cross-cutting incidents and reusable mitigation strategies to assist in inter-community response.	The type of information shared by coordinating teams with their counterparts often consists of periodical summaries during "steady state" operations, punctuated by the exchange of tactical, technical details, response plans, and impact or risk assessment information during coordinated incident response activities.

Organizations may find it challenging to build the relationships needed for coordination. Good places to start building a community include the industry sector that the organization belongs to and the geographic region where the organization operates. An organization's incident response team can try to form relationships with other teams (at the team-to-team level) within its own industry sector and region, or join established bodies within the industry sector that already facilitate information sharing. Another consideration for building relationships is that some relationships are mandatory and others voluntary; for example, team-to-coordinating team relationships are often mandatory, while team-to-team relationships are usually voluntary. Organizations pursue voluntary relationships because they fulfill mutual self-interests. Mandatory relationships are usually defined by a regulatory body within the industry or by another entity.

4.1.2 Sharing Agreements and Reporting Requirements

Organizations trying to share information with external organizations should consult with their legal department before initiating any coordination efforts. There may be contracts or other agreements that need to be put into place before discussions occur. An example is a nondisclosure agreement (NDA) to protect the confidentiality of the organization's most sensitive information. Organizations should also consider any existing requirements for reporting, such as sharing incident information with an ISAC or reporting incidents to a higher-level CIRT.

4.2 Information Sharing Techniques

Information sharing is a key element of enabling coordination across organizations. Even the smallest organizations need to be able to share incident information with peers and partners in order to deal with many incidents effectively. Organizations should perform such information sharing throughout the incident response life cycle and not wait until an incident has been fully resolved before sharing details of it with others. Section 4.3 discusses the types of incident information that organizations may or may not want to share with others.

This section focuses on techniques for information sharing. Section 4.2.1 looks at ad hoc methods, while Section 4.2.2 examines partially automated methods. Finally, Section 4.2.3 discusses security considerations related to information sharing.

4.2.1 Ad Hoc

Most incident information sharing has traditionally occurred through ad hoc methods, such as email, instant messaging clients, and phone. Ad hoc information sharing mechanisms normally rely on an individual employee's connections with employees in incident response teams of partner organizations. The employee uses these connections to manually share information with peers and coordinate with them to construct strategies for responding to an incident. Depending on the size of the organization, these ad hoc techniques may be the most cost-effective way of sharing information with partner organizations. However, due to the informal nature of ad hoc information sharing, it is not possible to guarantee that the information sharing processes will always operate. For example, if a particularly well-connected employee resigns from an incident response team, that team may temporarily lose the majority of information sharing channels it relies on to effectively coordinate with outside organizations.

Ad hoc information sharing methods are also largely unstandardized in terms of what information is communicated and how that communication occurs. Because of the lack of standardization, they tend to require manual intervention and to be more resource-intensive to process than the alternative, partially automated methods. Whenever possible an organization should attempt to formalize its information sharing strategies through formal agreements with partner organizations and technical mechanisms that will help to partially automate the sharing of information.

4.2.2 Partially Automated

Organizations should attempt to automate as much of the information sharing process as possible to make cross-organizational coordination efficient and cost effective. In reality, it will not be possible to fully automate the sharing of all incident information, nor will it be desirable due to security and trust considerations. Organizations should attempt to achieve a balance of automated information sharing overlaid with human-centric processes for managing the information flow.

When engineering automated information sharing solutions, organizations should first consider what types of information they will communicate with partners. The organization may want to construct a formal data dictionary enumerating all entities and relationships between entities that they will wish to share. Once the organization understands the types of information they will share, it is necessary to construct formal, machine-processable models to capture this information. Wherever possible, an organization should use existing data exchange standards for representing the information they need to share.[47] The organization should work with its partner organizations when deciding on the data exchange models to ensure that the standards selected are compatible with the partner organization's incident response systems. When selecting existing data exchange models, organizations may prefer to select multiple models that model different aspects of the incident response domain and then leverage these models in a modular fashion, communicating only the information needed at a specific decision point in the life cycle. Appendix E provides a non-exhaustive list of existing standards defining data exchange models that are applicable to the incident response domain.

In addition to selecting the data exchange models for sharing incident information, an organization must also work with its partner organizations to agree on the technical transport mechanisms for enabling the information exchange to occur in an automated fashion. These transport mechanisms include, at a minimum, the transport protocol for exchanging the information, the architectural model for communicating with an information resource, and the applicable ports and domain names for accessing an information resource in a particular organization. For example, a group of partner organizations may decide to exchange incident information using a Representational State Transfer (REST) architecture to exchange IODEF/Real-Time Inter-Network Defense (RID) data over Hypertext Transfer Protocol Secure (HTTPS) on port 4590 of a specific domain name within each organization's DMZ.

4.2.3 Security Considerations

There are several security considerations that incident response teams should consider when planning their information sharing. One is being able to designate who can see which pieces of incident information (e.g., protection of sensitive information). It may also be necessary to perform data sanitization or scrubbing to remove sensitive pieces of data from the incident information without disturbing the information on precursors, indicators, and other technical information. See Section 4.3 for more information on granular information sharing. The incident response team should also ensure that the necessary measures are taken to protect information shared with the team by other organizations.

There are also many legal issues to consider regarding data sharing. See Section 4.1.2 for additional information.

4.3 Granular Information Sharing

Organizations need to balance the benefits of information sharing with the drawbacks of sharing sensitive information, ideally sharing the necessary information and only the necessary information with the appropriate parties. Organizations can think of their incident information as being comprised of two types of information: business impact and technical. Business impact information is often shared in the context of a team-to-coordinating-team relationship as defined in Section 4.1.1, while technical information is often shared within all three types of coordination relationships. This section discusses both types of information and provides recommendations for performing granular information sharing.

4.3.1 Business Impact Information

Business impact information involves how the incident is affecting the organization in terms of mission impact, financial impact, etc. Such information, at least at a summary level, is often reported to higher-level coordinating incident response teams to communicate an estimate of the damage caused by the incident. Coordinating response teams may need this impact information to make decisions regarding the

---

[47] According to the National Technology Transfer and Advancement Act (NTTAA), "all Federal agencies and departments shall use technical standards that are developed or adopted by voluntary consensus standards bodies". See http://standards.gov/nttaa.cfm for more details.

degree of assistance to provide to the reporting organization. A coordinating team may also use this information to make decisions relative to how a specific incident will affect other organizations in the community they represent.

Coordinating teams may require member organizations to report on some degree of business impact information. For example, a coordinating team may require a member organization to report impact information using the categories defined in Section 3.2.6. In this case, for a hypothetical incident an organization would report that it has a functional impact of *medium*, an information impact of *none*, and will require *extended* recoverability time. This high-level information would alert the coordinating team that the member organization requires some level of additional resources to recover from the incident. The coordinating team could then pursue additional communication with the member organization to determine how many resources are required as well as the type of resources based on the technical information provided about the incident.

Business impact information is only useful for reporting to organizations that have some interest in ensuring the mission of the organization experiencing the incident. In many cases, incident response teams should avoid sharing business impact information with outside organizations unless there is a clear value proposition or formal reporting requirements. When sharing information with peer and partner organizations, incident response teams should focus on exchanging technical information as outlined in Section 4.3.2.

4.3.2 Technical Information

There are many different types of technical indicators signifying the occurrence of an incident within an organization. These indicators originate from the variety of technical information associated with incidents, such as the hostnames and IP addresses of attacking hosts, samples of malware, precursors and indicators of similar incidents, and types of vulnerabilities exploited in an incident. Section 3.2.2 provides an overview of how organizations should collect and utilize these indicators to help identify an incident that is in progress. In addition, Section 3.2.3 provides a listing of common sources of incident indicator data.

While organizations gain value from collecting their own internal indicators, they may gain additional value from analyzing indicators received from partner organizations and sharing internal indicators for external analysis and use. If the organization receives external indicator data pertaining to an incident they have not seen, they can use that indicator data to identify the incident as it begins to occur. Similarly, an organization may use external indicator data to detect an ongoing incident that it was not aware of due to the lack of internal resources to capture the specific indicator data. Organizations may also benefit from sharing their internal indicator data with external organizations. For example, if they share technical information pertaining to an incident they are experiencing, a partner organization may respond with a suggested remediation strategy for handling that incident.

Organizations should share as much of this information as possible; however, there may be both security and liability reasons why an organization would not want to reveal the details of an exploited vulnerability. External indicators, such as the general characteristics of attacks and the identity of attacking hosts, are usually safe to share with others. Organizations should consider which types of technical information should or should not be shared with various parties, and then endeavor to share as much of the appropriate information as possible with other organizations.

Technical indicator data is useful when it allows an organization to identify an actual incident. However, not all indicator data received from external sources will pertain to the organization receiving it. In some cases, this external data will generate false positives within the receiving organization's network and may cause resources to be spent on nonexistent problems.

Organizations participating in incident information sharing should have staff skilled in taking technical indicator information from sharing communities and disseminating that information throughout the enterprise, preferably in an automated way. Organizations should also attempt to ensure that they only share an indicator for which they have a relatively high level of confidence that it signifies an actual incident.

4.4 Recommendations

The key recommendations presented in this section for handling incidents are summarized below.

- **Plan incident coordination with external parties before incidents occur.** Examples of external parties include other incident response teams, law enforcement agencies, Internet service providers, and constituents and customers. This planning helps ensure that all parties know their roles and that effective lines of communication are established.
- **Consult with the legal department before initiating any coordination efforts.** There may be contracts or other agreements that need to be put into place before discussions occur.
- **Perform incident information sharing throughout the incident response life cycle.** Information sharing is a key element of enabling coordination across organizations. Organizations should not wait until an incident has been fully resolved before sharing details of it with others.
- **Attempt to automate as much of the information sharing process as possible.** This makes cross-organizational coordination efficient and cost effective. Organizations should attempt to achieve a balance of automated information sharing overlaid with human-centric processes for managing the information flow.
- **Balance the benefits of information sharing with the drawbacks of sharing sensitive information.** Ideally organizations should share the necessary information and only the necessary information with the appropriate parties. Business impact information is often shared in a team-to-coordinating team relationship, while technical information is often shared within all types of coordination relationships. When sharing information with peer and partner organizations, incident response teams should focus on exchanging technical information.
- **Share as much of the appropriate incident information as possible with other organizations.** Organizations should consider which types of technical information should or should not be shared with various parties. For example, external indicators, such as the general characteristics of attacks and the identity of attacking hosts, are usually safe to share with others, but there may be both security and liability reasons why an organization would not want to reveal the details of an exploited vulnerability.

Appendix A—Incident Handling Scenarios

Incident handling scenarios provide an inexpensive and effective way to build incident response skills and identify potential issues with incident response processes. The incident response team or team members are presented with a scenario and a list of related questions. The team then discusses each question and determines the most likely answer. The goal is to determine what the team would really do and to compare that with policies, procedures, and generally recommended practices to identify discrepancies or deficiencies. For example, the answer to one question may indicate that the response would be delayed because the team lacks a piece of software or because another team does not provide off-hours support.

The questions listed below are applicable to almost any scenario. Each question is followed by a reference to the related section(s) of the document. After the questions are scenarios, each of which is followed by additional incident-specific questions. Organizations are strongly encouraged to adapt these questions and scenarios for use in their own incident response exercises.[48]

A.1 Scenario Questions

Preparation:

1. Would the organization consider this activity to be an incident? If so, which of the organization's policies does this activity violate? *(Section 2.1)*
2. What measures are in place to attempt to prevent this type of incident from occurring or to limit its impact? *(Section 3.1.2)*

Detection and Analysis:

1. What precursors of the incident, if any, might the organization detect? Would any precursors cause the organization to take action before the incident occurred? *(Sections 3.2.2, 3.2.3)*
2. What indicators of the incident might the organization detect? Which indicators would cause someone to think that an incident might have occurred? *(Sections 3.2.2, 3.2.3)*
3. What additional tools might be needed to detect this particular incident? *(Section 3.2.3)*
4. How would the incident response team analyze and validate this incident? What personnel would be involved in the analysis and validation process? *(Section 3.2.4)*
5. To which people and groups within the organization would the team report the incident? *(Section 3.2.7)*
6. How would the team prioritize the handling of this incident? *(Section 3.2.6)*

Containment, Eradication, and Recovery:

1. What strategy should the organization take to contain the incident? Why is this strategy preferable to others? *(Section 3.3.1)*
2. What could happen if the incident were not contained? *(Section 3.3.1)*
3. What additional tools might be needed to respond to this particular incident? *(Sections 3.3.1, 3.3.4)*
4. Which personnel would be involved in the containment, eradication, and/or recovery processes? *(Sections 3.3.1, 3.3.4)*

---

48 For additional information on exercises, see NIST SP 800-84, *Guide to Test, Training, and Exercise Programs for IT Plans and Capabilities*, which is available at http://csrc nist.gov/publications/PubsSPs html#800-84.

5. What sources of evidence, if any, should the organization acquire? How would the evidence be acquired? Where would it be stored? How long should it be retained? *(Sections 3.2.5, 3.3.2, 3.4.3)*

Post-Incident Activity:

1. Who would attend the lessons learned meeting regarding this incident? *(Section 3.4.1)*
2. What could be done to prevent similar incidents from occurring in the future? *(Section 3.1.2)*
3. What could be done to improve detection of similar incidents? *(Section 3.1.2)*

General Questions:

1. How many incident response team members would participate in handling this incident? *(Section 2.4.3)*
2. Besides the incident response team, what groups within the organization would be involved in handling this incident? *(Section 2.4.4)*
3. To which external parties would the team report the incident? When would each report occur? How would each report be made? What information would you report or not report, and why? *(Section 2.3.2)*
4. What other communications with external parties may occur? *(Section 2.3.2)*
5. What tools and resources would the team use in handling this incident? *(Section 3.1.1)*
6. What aspects of the handling would have been different if the incident had occurred at a different day and time (on-hours versus off-hours)? *(Section 2.4.2)*
7. What aspects of the handling would have been different if the incident had occurred at a different physical location (onsite versus offsite)? *(Section 2.4.2)*

A.2 Scenarios

Scenario 1: Domain Name System (DNS) Server Denial of Service (DoS)

On a Saturday afternoon, external users start having problems accessing the organization's public websites. Over the next hour, the problem worsens to the point where nearly every access attempt fails. Meanwhile, a member of the organization's networking staff responds to alerts from an Internet border router and determines that the organization's Internet bandwidth is being consumed by an unusually large volume of User Datagram Protocol (UDP) packets to and from both the organization's public DNS servers. Analysis of the traffic shows that the DNS servers are receiving high volumes of requests from a single external IP address. Also, all the DNS requests from that address come from the same source port.

The following are additional questions for this scenario:

1. Whom should the organization contact regarding the external IP address in question?
2. Suppose that after the initial containment measures were put in place, the network administrators detected that nine internal hosts were also attempting the same unusual requests to the DNS server. How would that affect the handling of this incident?
3. Suppose that two of the nine internal hosts disconnected from the network before their system owners were identified. How would the system owners be identified?

Scenario 2: Worm and Distributed Denial of Service (DDoS) Agent Infestation

On a Tuesday morning, a new worm is released; it spreads itself through removable media, and it can copy itself to open Windows shares. When the worm infects a host, it installs a DDoS agent. The organization has already incurred widespread infections before antivirus signatures become available several hours after the worm started to spread.

The following are additional questions for this scenario:

1. How would the incident response team identify all infected hosts?
2. How would the organization attempt to prevent the worm from entering the organization before antivirus signatures were released?
3. How would the organization attempt to prevent the worm from being spread by infected hosts before antivirus signatures were released?
4. Would the organization attempt to patch all vulnerable machines? If so, how would this be done?
5. How would the handling of this incident change if infected hosts that had received the DDoS agent had been configured to attack another organization's website the next morning?
6. How would the handling of this incident change if one or more of the infected hosts contained sensitive personally identifiable information regarding the organization's employees?
7. How would the incident response team keep the organization's users informed about the status of the incident?
8. What additional measures would the team perform for hosts that are not currently connected to the network (e.g., staff members on vacation, offsite employees who connect occasionally)?

Scenario 3: Stolen Documents

On a Monday morning, the organization's legal department receives a call from the Federal Bureau of Investigation (FBI) regarding some suspicious activity involving the organization's systems. Later that day, an FBI agent meets with members of management and the legal department to discuss the activity. The FBI has been investigating activity involving public posting of sensitive government documents, and some of the documents reportedly belong to the organization. The agent asks for the organization's assistance, and management asks for the incident response team's assistance in acquiring the necessary evidence to determine if these documents are legitimate or not and how they might have been leaked.

The following are additional questions for this scenario:

1. From what sources might the incident response team gather evidence?
2. What would the team do to keep the investigation confidential?
3. How would the handling of this incident change if the team identified an internal host responsible for the leaks?
4. How would the handling of this incident change if the team found a rootkit installed on the internal host responsible for the leaks?

Scenario 4: Compromised Database Server

On a Tuesday night, a database administrator performs some off-hours maintenance on several production database servers. The administrator notices some unfamiliar and unusual directory names on one of the servers. After reviewing the directory listings and viewing some of the files, the administrator concludes that the server has been attacked and calls the incident response team for assistance. The team's investigation determines that the attacker successfully gained root access to the server six weeks ago.

The following are additional questions for this scenario:

1. What sources might the team use to determine when the compromise had occurred?

2. How would the handling of this incident change if the team found that the database server had been running a packet sniffer and capturing passwords from the network?
3. How would the handling of this incident change if the team found that the server was running a process that would copy a database containing sensitive customer information (including personally identifiable information) each night and transfer it to an external address?
4. How would the handling of this incident change if the team discovered a rootkit on the server?

Scenario 5: Unknown Exfiltration

On a Sunday night, one of the organization's network intrusion detection sensors alerts on anomalous outbound network activity involving large file transfers. The intrusion analyst reviews the alerts; it appears that thousands of .RAR files are being copied from an internal host to an external host, and the external host is located in another country. The analyst contacts the incident response team so that it can investigate the activity further. The team is unable to see what the .RAR files hold because their contents are encrypted. Analysis of the internal host containing the .RAR files shows signs of a bot installation.

The following are additional questions for this scenario:

1. How would the team determine what was most likely inside the .RAR files? Which other teams might assist the incident response team?
2. If the incident response team determined that the initial compromise had been performed through a wireless network card in the internal host, how would the team further investigate this activity?
3. If the incident response team determined that the internal host was being used to stage sensitive files from other hosts within the enterprise, how would the team further investigate this activity?

Scenario 6: Unauthorized Access to Payroll Records

On a Wednesday evening, the organization's physical security team receives a call from a payroll administrator who saw an unknown person leave her office, run down the hallway, and exit the building. The administrator had left her workstation unlocked and unattended for only a few minutes. The payroll program is still logged in and on the main menu, as it was when she left it, but the administrator notices that the mouse appears to have been moved. The incident response team has been asked to acquire evidence related to the incident and to determine what actions were performed.

The following are additional questions for this scenario:

1. How would the team determine what actions had been performed?
2. How would the handling of this incident differ if the payroll administrator had recognized the person leaving her office as a former payroll department employee?
3. How would the handling of this incident differ if the team had reason to believe that the person was a current employee?
4. How would the handling of this incident differ if the physical security team determined that the person had used social engineering techniques to gain physical access to the building?
5. How would the handling of this incident differ if logs from the previous week showed an unusually large number of failed remote login attempts using the payroll administrator's user ID?
6. How would the handling of this incident differ if the incident response team discovered that a keystroke logger was installed on the computer two weeks earlier?

Scenario 7: Disappearing Host

On a Thursday afternoon, a network intrusion detection sensor records vulnerability scanning activity directed at internal hosts that is being generated by an internal IP address. Because the intrusion detection analyst is unaware of any authorized, scheduled vulnerability scanning activity, she reports the activity to the incident response team. When the team begins the analysis, it discovers that the activity has stopped and that there is no longer a host using the IP address.

The following are additional questions for this scenario:

1. What data sources might contain information regarding the identity of the vulnerability scanning host?
2. How would the team identify who had been performing the vulnerability scans?
3. How would the handling of this incident differ if the vulnerability scanning were directed at the organization's most critical hosts?
4. How would the handling of this incident differ if the vulnerability scanning were directed at external hosts?
5. How would the handling of this incident differ if the internal IP address was associated with the organization's wireless guest network?
6. How would the handling of this incident differ if the physical security staff discovered that someone had broken into the facility half an hour before the vulnerability scanning occurred?

Scenario 8: Telecommuting Compromise

On a Saturday night, network intrusion detection software records an inbound connection originating from a watchlist IP address. The intrusion detection analyst determines that the connection is being made to the organization's VPN server and contacts the incident response team. The team reviews the intrusion detection, firewall, and VPN server logs and identifies the user ID that was authenticated for the session and the name of the user associated with the user ID.

The following are additional questions for this scenario:

1. What should the team's next step be (e.g., calling the user at home, disabling the user ID, disconnecting the VPN session)? Why should this step be performed first? What step should be performed second?
2. How would the handling of this incident differ if the external IP address belonged to an open proxy?
3. How would the handling of this incident differ if the ID had been used to initiate VPN connections from several external IP addresses without the knowledge of the user?
4. Suppose that the identified user's computer had become compromised by a game containing a Trojan horse that was downloaded by a family member. How would this affect the team's analysis of the incident? How would this affect evidence gathering and handling? What should the team do in terms of eradicating the incident from the user's computer?
5. Suppose that the user installed antivirus software and determined that the Trojan horse had included a keystroke logger. How would this affect the handling of the incident? How would this affect the handling of the incident if the user were a system administrator? How would this affect the handling of the incident if the user were a high-ranking executive in the organization?

Scenario 9: Anonymous Threat

On a Thursday afternoon, the organization's physical security team receives a call from an IT manager, reporting that two of her employees just received anonymous threats against the organization's systems. Based on an investigation, the physical security team believes that the threats should be taken seriously and notifies the appropriate internal teams, including the incident response team, of the threats.

The following are additional questions for this scenario:

1. What should the incident response team do differently, if anything, in response to the notification of the threats?
2. What impact could heightened physical security controls have on the team's responses to incidents?

Scenario 10: Peer-to-Peer File Sharing

The organization prohibits the use of peer-to-peer file sharing services. The organization's network intrusion detection sensors have signatures enabled that can detect the usage of several popular peer-to-peer file sharing services. On a Monday evening, an intrusion detection analyst notices that several file sharing alerts have occurred during the past three hours, all involving the same internal IP address.

1. What factors should be used to prioritize the handling of this incident (e.g., the apparent content of the files that are being shared)?
2. What privacy considerations may impact the handling of this incident?
3. How would the handling of this incident differ if the computer performing peer-to-peer file sharing also contains sensitive personally identifiable information?

Scenario 11: Unknown Wireless Access Point

On a Monday morning, the organization's help desk receives calls from three users on the same floor of a building who state that they are having problems with their wireless access. A network administrator who is asked to assist in resolving the problem brings a laptop with wireless access to the users' floor. As he views his wireless networking configuration, he notices that there is a new access point listed as being available. He checks with his teammates and determines that this access point was not deployed by his team, so that it is most likely a rogue access point that was established without permission.

1. What should be the first major step in handling this incident (e.g., physically finding the rogue access point, logically attaching to the access point)?
2. What is the fastest way to locate the access point? What is the most covert way to locate the access point?
3. How would the handling of this incident differ if the access point had been deployed by an external party (e.g., contractor) temporarily working at the organization's office?
4. How would the handling of this incident differ if an intrusion detection analyst reported signs of suspicious activity involving some of the workstations on the same floor of the building?
5. How would the handling of this incident differ if the access point had been removed while the team was still attempting to physically locate it?

Appendix B—Incident-Related Data Elements

Organizations should identify a standard set of incident-related data elements to be collected for each incident. This effort will not only facilitate more effective and consistent incident handling, but also assist the organization in meeting applicable incident reporting requirements. The organization should designate a set of basic elements (e.g., incident reporter's name, phone number, and location) to be collected when the incident is reported and an additional set of elements to be collected by the incident handlers during their response. The two sets of elements would be the basis for the incident reporting database, previously discussed in Section 3.2.5. The lists below provide suggestions of what information to collect for incidents and are not intended to be comprehensive. Each organization should create its own list of elements based on several factors, including its incident response team model and structure and its definition of the term "incident."

B.1 Basic Data Elements

- Contact Information for the Incident Reporter and Handler
  - Name
  - Role
  - Organizational unit (e.g., agency, department, division, team) and affiliation
  - Email address
  - Phone number
  - Location (e.g., mailing address, office room number)
- Incident Details
  - Status change date/timestamps (including time zone): when the incident started, when the incident was discovered/detected, when the incident was reported, when the incident was resolved/ended, etc.
  - Physical location of the incident (e.g., city, state)
  - Current status of the incident (e.g., ongoing attack)
  - Source/cause of the incident (if known), including hostnames and IP addresses
  - Description of the incident (e.g., how it was detected, what occurred)
  - Description of affected resources (e.g., networks, hosts, applications, data), including systems' hostnames, IP addresses, and function
  - If known, incident category, vectors of attack associated with the incident, and indicators related to the incident (traffic patterns, registry keys, etc.)
  - Prioritization factors (functional impact, information impact, recoverability, etc.)
  - Mitigating factors (e.g., stolen laptop containing sensitive data was using full disk encryption)
  - Response actions performed (e.g., shut off host, disconnected host from network)
  - Other organizations contacted (e.g., software vendor)
- General Comments

B.2 Incident Handler Data Elements

- Current Status of the Incident Response
- Summary of the Incident
- Incident Handling Actions
  - Log of actions taken by all handlers
  - Contact information for all involved parties
  - List of evidence gathered
- Incident Handler Comments
- Cause of the Incident (e.g., misconfigured application, unpatched host)
- Cost of the Incident
- Business Impact of the Incident[49]

[49] The business impact of the incident could either be a description of the incident's effect (e.g., accounting department unable to perform tasks for two days) or an impact category based on the cost (e.g., a "major" incident has a cost of over $100,000).

Appendix C—Glossary

Selected terms used in the publication are defined below.

Baselining: Monitoring resources to determine typical utilization patterns so that significant deviations can be detected.

Computer Security Incident: See "incident."

Computer Security Incident Response Team (CSIRT): A capability set up for the purpose of assisting in responding to computer security-related incidents; also called a Computer Incident Response Team (CIRT) or a CIRC (Computer Incident Response Center, Computer Incident Response Capability).

Event: Any observable occurrence in a network or system.

False Positive: An alert that incorrectly indicates that malicious activity is occurring.

Incident: A violation or imminent threat of violation of computer security policies, acceptable use policies, or standard security practices.

Incident Handling: The mitigation of violations of security policies and recommended practices.

Incident Response: See "incident handling."

Indicator: A sign that an incident may have occurred or may be currently occurring.

Intrusion Detection and Prevention System (IDPS): Software that automates the process of monitoring the events occurring in a computer system or network and analyzing them for signs of possible incidents and attempting to stop detected possible incidents.

Malware: A virus, worm, Trojan horse, or other code-based malicious entity that successfully infects a host.

Precursor: A sign that an attacker may be preparing to cause an incident.

Profiling: Measuring the characteristics of expected activity so that changes to it can be more easily identified.

Signature: A recognizable, distinguishing pattern associated with an attack, such as a binary string in a virus or a particular set of keystrokes used to gain unauthorized access to a system.

Social Engineering: An attempt to trick someone into revealing information (e.g., a password) that can be used to attack systems or networks.

Threat: The potential source of an adverse event.

Vulnerability: A weakness in a system, application, or network that is subject to exploitation or misuse.

Appendix D—Acronyms

Selected acronyms used in the publication are defined below.

CCIPS	Computer Crime and Intellectual Property Section
CERIAS	Center for Education and Research in Information Assurance and Security
CERT®/CC	CERT® Coordination Center
CIO	Chief Information Officer
CIRC	Computer Incident Response Capability
CIRC	Computer Incident Response Center
CIRT	Computer Incident Response Team
CISO	Chief Information Security Officer
CSIRC	Computer Security Incident Response Capability
CSIRT	Computer Security Incident Response Team
DDoS	Distributed Denial of Service
DHS	Department of Homeland Security
DNS	Domain Name System
DoS	Denial of Service
FAQ	Frequently Asked Questions
FBI	Federal Bureau of Investigation
FIPS	Federal Information Processing Standards
FIRST	Forum of Incident Response and Security Teams
FISMA	Federal Information Security Management Act
GAO	General Accountability Office
GFIRST	Government Forum of Incident Response and Security Teams
GRS	General Records Schedule
HTTP	HyperText Transfer Protocol
IANA	Internet Assigned Numbers Authority
IDPS	Intrusion Detection and Prevention System
IETF	Internet Engineering Task Force
IP	Internet Protocol
IR	Interagency Report
IRC	Internet Relay Chat
ISAC	Information Sharing and Analysis Center
ISP	Internet Service Provider
IT	Information Technology
ITL	Information Technology Laboratory
MAC	Media Access Control
MOU	Memorandum of Understanding
MSSP	Managed Security Services Provider
NAT	Network Address Translation
NDA	Non-Disclosure Agreement
NIST	National Institute of Standards and Technology
NSRL	National Software Reference Library
NTP	Network Time Protocol
NVD	National Vulnerability Database
OIG	Office of Inspector General
OMB	Office of Management and Budget
OS	Operating System
PII	Personally Identifiable Information
PIN	Personal Identification Number

POC	Point of Contact
REN-ISAC	Research and Education Networking Information Sharing and Analysis Center
RFC	Request for Comment
RID	Real-Time Inter-Network Defense
SIEM	Security Information and Event Management
SLA	Service Level Agreement
SOP	Standard Operating Procedure
SP	Special Publication
TCP	Transmission Control Protocol
TCP/IP	Transmission Control Protocol/Internet Protocol
TERENA	Trans-European Research and Education Networking Association
UDP	User Datagram Protocol
URL	Uniform Resource Locator
US-CERT	United States Computer Emergency Readiness Team
VPN	Virtual Private Network

Appendix E—Resources

The lists below provide examples of resources that may be helpful in establishing and maintaining an incident response capability.

Incident Response Organizations

Organization	URL
Anti-Phishing Working Group (APWG)	http://www.antiphishing.org/
Computer Crime and Intellectual Property Section (CCIPS), U.S. Department of Justice	http://www.cybercrime.gov/
CERT® Coordination Center, Carnegie Mellon University (CERT®/CC)	http://www.cert.org/
European Network and Information Security Agency (ENISA)	http://www.enisa.europa.eu/activities/cert
Forum of Incident Response and Security Teams (FIRST)	http://www.first.org/
Government Forum of Incident Response and Security Teams (GFIRST)	http://www.us-cert.gov/federal/gfirst.html
High Technology Crime Investigation Association (HTCIA)	http://www.htcia.org/
InfraGard	http://www.infragard.net/
Internet Storm Center (ISC)	http://isc.sans.edu/
National Council of ISACs	http://www.isaccouncil.org/
United States Computer Emergency Response Team (US-CERT)	http://www.us-cert.gov/

NIST Publications

Resource Name	URL
NIST SP 800-53 Revision 3, *Recommended Security Controls for Federal Information Systems and Organizations*	http://csrc.nist.gov/publications/PubsSPs.html#800-53
NIST SP 800-83, *Guide to Malware Incident Prevention and Handling*	http://csrc.nist.gov/publications/PubsSPs.html#800-83
NIST SP 800-84, *Guide to Test, Training, and Exercise Programs for IT Plans and Capabilities*	http://csrc.nist.gov/publications/PubsSPs.html#800-84
NIST SP 800-86, *Guide to Integrating Forensic Techniques into Incident Response*	http://csrc.nist.gov/publications/PubsSPs.html#800-86
NIST SP 800-92, *Guide to Computer Security Log Management*	http://csrc.nist.gov/publications/PubsSPs.html#800-92
NIST SP 800-94, *Guide to Intrusion Detection and Prevention Systems (IDPS)*	http://csrc.nist.gov/publications/PubsSPs.html#800-94
NIST SP 800-115, *Technical Guide to Information Security Testing and Assessment*	http://csrc.nist.gov/publications/PubsSPs.html#800-115
NIST SP 800-128, *Guide for Security-Focused Configuration Management of Information Systems*	http://csrc.nist.gov/publications/PubsSPs.html#800-128

Data Exchange Specifications Applicable to Incident Handling

Title	Description	Additional Information
AI	Asset Identification	http://csrc.nist.gov/publications/ PubsNISTIRs.html#NIST-IR-7693
ARF	Asset Results Format	http://csrc.nist.gov/publications/ PubsNISTIRs.html#NIST-IR-7694
CAPEC	Common Attack Pattern Enumeration and Classification	http://capec.mitre.org/
CCE	Common Configuration Enumeration	http://cce.mitre.org/
CEE	Common Event Expression	http://cee.mitre.org/
CPE	Common Platform Enumeration	http://cpe.mitre.org/
CVE	Common Vulnerabilities and Exposures	http://cve.mitre.org/
CVSS	Common Vulnerability Scoring System	http://www.first.org/cvss/cvss-guide
CWE	Common Weakness Enumeration	http://cwe.mitre.org/
CybOX	Cyber Observable eXpression	http://cybox.mitre.org/
MAEC	Malware Attribute Enumeration and Characterization	http://maec.mitre.org/
OCIL	Open Checklist Interactive Language	http://csrc.nist.gov/publications/ PubsNISTIRs.html#NIST-IR-7692
OVAL	Open Vulnerability Assessment Language	http://oval.mitre.org/
RFC 4765	Intrusion Detection Message Exchange Format (IDMEF)	http://www.ietf.org/rfc/rfc4765.txt
RFC 5070	Incident Object Description Exchange Format (IODEF)	http://www.ietf.org/rfc/rfc5070.txt
RFC 5901	Extensions to the IODEF for Reporting Phishing	http://www.ietf.org/rfc/rfc5901.txt
RFC 5941	Sharing Transaction Fraud Data	http://www.ietf.org/rfc/rfc5941.txt
RFC 6545	Real-time Inter-network Defense (RID)	http://www.ietf.org/rfc/rfc6545.txt
RFC 6546	Transport of Real-time Inter-network Defense (RID) Messages over HTTP/TLS	http://www.ietf.org/rfc/rfc6546.txt
SCAP	Security Content Automation Protocol	http://csrc.nist.gov/publications/PubsSPs.html #SP-800-126-Rev.%202
XCCDF	Extensible Configuration Checklist Description Format	http://csrc.nist.gov/publications/ PubsNISTIRs.html#NIST-IR-7275-r4

Appendix F—Frequently Asked Questions

Users, system administrators, information security staff members, and others within organizations may have questions about incident response. The following are frequently asked questions (FAQ). Organizations are encouraged to customize this FAQ and make it available to their user community.

1. **What is an incident?**

   In general, an incident is a violation of computer security policies, acceptable use policies, or standard computer security practices. Examples of incidents are:

   - An attacker commands a botnet to send high volumes of connection requests to one of an organization's web servers, causing it to crash.
   - Users are tricked into opening a "quarterly report" sent via email that is actually malware; running the tool has infected their computers and established connections with an external host.
   - A perpetrator obtains unauthorized access to sensitive data and threatens to release the details to the press if the organization does not pay a designated sum of money.
   - A user provides illegal copies of software to others through peer-to-peer file sharing services.

2. **What is incident handling?**

   Incident handling is the process of detecting and analyzing incidents and limiting the incident's effect. For example, if an attacker breaks into a system through the Internet, the incident handling process should detect the security breach. Incident handlers will then analyze the data and determine how serious the attack is. The incident will be prioritized, and the incident handlers will take action to ensure that the progress of the incident is halted and that the affected systems return to normal operation as soon as possible.

3. **What is incident response?**

   The terms "incident handling" and "incident response" are synonymous in this document.[50]

4. **What is an incident response team?**

   An incident response team (also known as a Computer Security Incident Response Team [CSIRT]) is responsible for providing incident response services to part or all of an organization. The team receives information on possible incidents, investigates them, and takes action to ensure that the damage caused by the incidents is minimized.

5. **What services does the incident response team provide?**

   The particular services that incident response teams offer vary widely among organizations. Besides performing incident handling, most teams also assume responsibility for intrusion detection system monitoring and management. A team may also distribute advisories regarding new threats, and educate users and IT staff on their roles in incident prevention and handling.

6. **To whom should incidents be reported?**

   Organizations should establish clear points of contact (POC) for reporting incidents internally. Some organizations will structure their incident response capability so that all incidents are reported directly to the incident response team, whereas others will use existing support

---

50 Definitions of "incident handling" and "incident response" vary widely. For example, CERT®/CC uses "incident handling" to refer to the overall process of incident detection, reporting, analysis, and response, whereas "incident response" refers specifically to incident containment, recovery, and notification of others. See http://www.cert.org/csirts/csirt_faq.html for more information.

structures, such as the IT help desk, for an initial POC. The organization should recognize that external parties, such as other incident response teams, would report some incidents. Federal agencies are required under the law to report all incidents to the United States Computer Emergency Readiness Team (US-CERT). All organizations are encouraged to report incidents to their appropriate Computer Security Incident Response Teams (CSIRTs). If an organization does not have its own CSIRT to contact, it can report incidents to other organizations, including Information Sharing and Analysis Centers (ISACs).

7. **How are incidents reported?**

Most organizations have multiple methods for reporting an incident. Different reporting methods may be preferable as a result of variations in the skills of the person reporting the activity, the urgency of the incident, and the sensitivity of the incident. A phone number should be established to report emergencies. An email address may be provided for informal incident reporting, whereas a web-based form may be useful in formal incident reporting. Sensitive information can be provided to the team by using a public key published by the team to encrypt the material.

8. **What information should be provided when reporting an incident?**

The more precise the information is, the better. For example, if a workstation appears to have been infected by malware, the incident report should include as much of the following data as practical:

- The user's name, user ID, and contact information (e.g., phone number, email address)
- The workstation's location, model number, serial number, hostname, and IP address
- The date and time that the incident occurred
- A step-by-step explanation of what happened, including what was done to the workstation after the infection was discovered. This explanation should be detailed, including the exact wording of messages, such as those displayed by the malware or by antivirus software alerts.

9. **How quickly does the incident response team respond to an incident report?**

The response time depends on several factors, such as the type of incident, the criticality of the resources and data that are affected, the severity of the incident, existing Service Level Agreements (SLA) for affected resources, the time and day of the week, and other incidents that the team is handling. Generally, the highest priority is handling incidents that are likely to cause the most damage to the organization or to other organizations.

10. **When should a person involved with an incident contact law enforcement?**

Communications with law enforcement agencies should be initiated by the incident response team members, the chief information officer (CIO), or other designated official—users, system administrators, system owners, and other involved parties should not initiate contact.

11. **What should someone do who discovers that a system has been attacked?**

The person should immediately stop using the system and contact the incident response team. The person may need to assist in the initial handling of the incident—for instance, physically monitoring the system until incident handlers arrive to protect evidence on the system.

12. **What should someone do who is contacted by the media regarding an incident?**

A person may answer the media's questions in accordance with the organization's policy regarding incidents and outside parties. If the person is not qualified to represent the organization in terms of discussing the incident, the person should make no comment regarding the incident, other than to refer the caller to the organization's public affairs office. This will allow the public affairs office to provide accurate and consistent information to the media and the public.

Appendix G—Crisis Handling Steps

This is a list of the major steps that should be performed when a technical professional believes that a serious incident has occurred and the organization does not have an incident response capability available. This serves as a basic reference of what to do for someone who is faced with a crisis and does not have time to read through this entire document.

1. **Document everything.** This effort includes every action that is performed, every piece of evidence, and every conversation with users, system owners, and others regarding the incident.
2. **Find a coworker who can provide assistance.** Handling the incident will be much easier if two or more people work together. For example, one person can perform actions while the other documents them.
3. **Analyze the evidence to confirm that an incident has occurred.** Perform additional research as necessary (e.g., Internet search engines, software documentation) to better understand the evidence. Reach out to other technical professionals within the organization for additional help.
4. **Notify the appropriate people within the organization.** This should include the chief information officer (CIO), the head of information security, and the local security manager. Use discretion when discussing details of an incident with others; tell only the people who need to know and use communication mechanisms that are reasonably secure. (If the attacker has compromised email services, do not send emails about the incident.)
5. **Notify US-CERT and/or other external organizations** for assistance in dealing with the incident.
6. **Stop the incident if it is still in progress.** The most common way to do this is to disconnect affected systems from the network. In some cases, firewall and router configurations may need to be modified to stop network traffic that is part of an incident, such as a denial of service (DoS) attack.
7. **Preserve evidence from the incident.** Make backups (preferably disk image backups, not file system backups) of affected systems. Make copies of log files that contain evidence related to the incident.
8. **Wipe out all effects of the incident.** This effort includes malware infections, inappropriate materials (e.g., pirated software), Trojan horse files, and any other changes made to systems by incidents. If a system has been fully compromised, rebuild it from scratch or restore it from a known good backup.
9. **Identify and mitigate all vulnerabilities that were exploited.** The incident may have occurred by taking advantage of vulnerabilities in operating systems or applications. It is critical to identify such vulnerabilities and eliminate or otherwise mitigate them so that the incident does not recur.
10. **Confirm that operations have been restored to normal.** Make sure that data, applications, and other services affected by the incident have been returned to normal operations.
11. **Create a final report.** This report should detail the incident handling process. It also should provide an executive summary of what happened and how a formal incident response capability would have helped to handle the situation, mitigate the risk, and limit the damage more quickly.

Appendix H—Change Log

Revision 2 Draft 1—January 2012

Editorial:

- Tightened writing throughout publication
- Made minor formatting changes throughout publication

Technical Changes:

- Expanded material on information sharing (throughout Section 2)
- Updated incident reporting organization listings (Section 2.3.4.3)
- Updated list of common incident response team services (Section 2.5)
- Revised the incident response life cycle diagrams (throughout Section 3)
- Revamped the list of attack vectors (Section 3.2.1)
- Revamped the factors for incident handling prioritization (Section 3.2.6)
- Changed focus from identifying the attacker to identifying the attacking host (Section 3.3.3)
- Expanded the list of possible incident metrics (Section 3.4.2)
- Updated the incident handling scenarios to reflect current threats (old Appendix B, new Appendix A)
- Made minor updates to incident-related data field suggestions (old Appendix C, new Appendix B)
- Updated all of the tools and resources listings (old Appendix G, new Appendix E)
- Updated the Frequently Asked Questions and the Crisis Handling Steps to reflect changes made elsewhere in the publication (old Appendices H and I, new Appendices F and G)

Deletions:

- Removed duplicate material on forensics, pointed readers to SP 800-86 for the same information (Section 3.3.2)
- Deleted material specific to the old incident categories (Sections 4 through 8)
- Deleted the duplicate list of recommendations (old Appendix A)
- Deleted print resources list (old Appendix F)
- Deleted federal agency incident reporting categories (old Appendix J)

Revision 2 Final—August 2012

Editorial:

- Made minor revisions throughout publication

Technical Changes:

- Added information sharing as a team service (Section 2.5)
- Converted Table 3-1 into bulleted lists (Section 3.1.1)
- Added a mention of exercises (Section 3.1.1)
- Revised the attack vectors (formerly incident categories) (Section 3.2.1)

- Added SIEMs, network flows as common sources of precursors and indicators (Section 3.2.3)
- Expanded discussion of eradication and recovery (Section 3.3.4)
- Added a section on coordination and information sharing (Section 4)
- Added a table of data exchange specifications applicable to incident handling (Appendix E)

www.ingramcontent.com/pod-product-compliance
Lightning Source LLC
Chambersburg PA
CBHW060458060326
40689CB00020B/4571
9781497468030